LET'S GO OUT AGAIN

INTERIORS FOR RESTAURANTS,
BARS AND
UNUSUAL FOOD PLACES

gestalten

LET'S GO OUT AGAIN

PREFACE

TEXT: SHONQUIS MORENO

While we are truly living in a consumer age, many of us are looking to consume less—literally, metaphorically, and environmentally. We strive to consume less "stuff" but of higher quality, and less food but of greater nutritional value. Eating spaces have become an extension of that simple ethos. Even the complexity of molecular cuisine has been countered with a renewed emphasis on simplicity, sustainability, authenticity, and craft (as opposed to science or art). And so we have been tapping into the do-it-yourself ethic, urban and indoor farming, artisanal butchery, distilling, and brewing. We are seeking out organic, healthy alternatives and once-in-a-lifetime culinary experiences. And we want them to be all-consuming.

In the following six chapters, we examine an eclectic selection of eating spaces from around the world through the prism of several aesthetic and conceptual points of view. These projects represent the collaborations taking place among architects, artists, designers, restaurateurs and chefs, a collusion targeted at all the senses and at our identities and values too. Each design approach works in tandem with the kitchen or bar that it serves, buoying and amplifying the philosophy practiced there. The result is a synergy between flavor and atmosphere, place and taste.

UNDERSTATED interiors are, by definition, refined and full of nuance—and they allow us, for a moment, to see ourselves in the same light. Without inserting itself into the conversation or cuisine, the space gives dimension to both. It manifests the making practiced behind the scenes or behind the bar, without hitting anyone over the palate with it. Creating this measured interior, however, involves finding balance, and simplifying without becoming simplistic. These aren't just one-size-fits-all spaces.

THE ARCADE BAKERY →P.34, for example, is masterfully balanced, with a streamlined design that never feels minimal. It isn't a whole-cloth piece of architecture, although it gives the impression of one; rather, it consists primarily of built-in furnishings. Mahogany plywood tables and seating are embedded in the walls, folding down from them and disappearing into them again after hours, as if they had never been there. ARCADE has a made-by-hand-when-everything-was-made-by-hand quality that stops short of nostalgia.

Instead of relying on frippery and garnishes, the projects collected in MODERN MUSINGS rely on truth to materials (as to ingredients), repetition, color, and, more than ever, texture. The popularity of this easygoing sensibility has to do with a renewed interest—in many areas of our lives, from food and technology to politics—in things that are transparent and easier to digest. The kitchen's philosophy of authenticity becomes a reason to burn the residual away, clarifying form and revealing the structure that lies beneath. What you see is what you get: these chefs abhor the superfluous, and the adulterated, and focus instead on a more democratic approach.

There are various means by which designers create "what you see is what you get" interiors. One method is to make the interior's structure and skin one and the same, the ultimate exposure. Long gone, however, are the days when we were thrilled by the faux exclusivity of minimal interiors that reflected the tiny portions of gourmet meals surrounded by a generous helping of blank white porcelain. Today's modern spaces usually look warm in spite of—and sometimes because of—this exposure. The JURY CAFE →P.52 consists of uncovered triangular plywood coffers. Partly painted, partly clear-finished, they look simultaneously naked and fully dressed, which makes every surface voyeuristically interesting. The old tenet of "truth to materials" assumes an updated meaning. Today, just as consumers must, designers ask: What are the implications of using these materials? Are they socially and ecologically responsible? What is sustainable?

Favored today are bold, natural materials like brass, copper, and marble, or crafted materials that bespeak comfort like glass, ceramics, and textiles. Many designers are increasingly throwing plants and potted succulents into the mix of interior design's "comfort foods" as well. They feel human-scale and humane. Take

THE ARCADE BAKERY →P.34
New York (NY), United States

JURY CAFE →P.52
Melbourne (VIC), Australia

5

HOG ISLAND OYSTER FARM →P.106
Marshall (CA), United States

character—a ship's wheel added here, a decommissioned fishing boat added there— they have created a work-in-progress that looks native to the bay's ecology. At the other end, these interiors are meticulously curated, their history pieced together by interior designers who are archaeologists as much as storytellers. Craft brewers brew the beer on the premises at SMOKESTACK AT MAGNOLIA BREWERY →P.108, a fact broadcast by the use of architectural salvage, wood paneling, and timber floors, which cultivate a saloon-like atmosphere.

PROGRESSIVE spaces take cues from innovations in anything from the kitchen or the architecture to the social fabric. They may be built around multimedia, multidisciplinary food, music, art, and design experiments. They often have an element of surprise, and challenge us to reconnect with creativity, with each other, and with the new or strange in real-time and in the flesh. Some are part of a nomadic, artistic food practice that longs—like many restaurant-goers—to be unfettered from the static nature and spatial, economic, social, and legal strictures of the conventional restaurant industry. Improvisation is seen as a source of innovation, not just in ways to cook and eat, but in uniting a tribe of people that might have coalesced only virtually or not at all. They may be problem-solving spaces, looking for new codes or freedom from old ones, that offer different flavors and fresh ways to eat, drink, listen, dance, or climb a jungle gym.

INFARM →P.140, for instance, is the latest manifestation of sustainable urban values that have taken root in the indoor farming movement. Its designers have transplanted these values into INFARM, which is both a café and a kitchen garden. Its walls hold growing vegetation attached to irrigation tubes and

MEAT LIQUOR BRIGHTON →P.196
Brighton, United Kingdom

hydroponics, recalling a cheerful lab experiment and creating a greenhouse for plants and people alike. The tower of metal monkey bars that is TADIOTO →P.146 is an experiment that asks: what more can eating space become if left to the whim of its users? A translation of the informal beer bars that spill into the streets

fashion designer Henrik Vibskov's DEN PLETTEDE GRIS →P.54 café, which consists of only elastic bands, wooden dowels, and a handful of paint colors. Sewn together, these limited threads give the space texture to the degree that the café itself comes to feel like a textile. It becomes an intimate, a cozy, and, yes, a minimal interior.

Today, we are seeking (a degree of) social transparency and agency, a sense of letting our hair down and rolling up our proverbial sleeves. We broadcast these values not just in what we consume, but in where and how we consume. The spaces in the ROUGH & LOCAL chapter, often rustic or industrial-retro, articulate the values of self-reliance, quality (but not superiority), and the authentic.

At either end of the spectrum, the rustic and industrial aesthetics can appear carpenterly and mechanical. But its timber-and-tile chic and workbench joinery are about making things well and making them (feel) real. They turn emphatically away from the aspirational interiors of the shelter magazines. At one extreme, they become stages of the authentic, compositions of objects salvaged from some actual history of their own in order to create a new one: tiles from a hundred-year-old charcuterie, or an ancient brass cash till. In combination, they create eating spaces that feel forthright, that settle deeply into their site and the menu, like an old house into its foundation. They look into the past with appreciation, but not slavishness.

At one end, these spaces develop organically. Time and use have carved them out in their passing. Over the years, the clapboard and picnic table–garnished HOG ISLAND OYSTER FARM →P.106 has been fleshed out naturally by its owners. By giving it a maritime-rustic

TADIOTO →P.146
Hanoi, Vietnam

6

of Hanoi, it is multilevel micro-architecture pedaled around behind a tricycle. Because it looks generic and doesn't announce its function, it has the potential to become any kind of social space that locals can imagine. Because color and graphics feed our senses and emotions, they are a fundamental tool in giving an eating place character. GRAPHIC SPACES evoke moods, and allow us, alcohol and drug-free, to fall safely under the influence. They don't necessarily advertise values and they're not necessarily about what's cooking in the kitchen. Instead, they create an immediate, emotional, and sometimes immersive experience, and viscerally connect people to the space and to each other.

Take the black box interiors of MEAT LIQUOR BRIGHTON →P.196 that Shed collaged with brawling, anarchic color and imagery from the nearby Brighton fairgrounds. They evoke a surreal place and create a seaside rollercoaster ride of sensory overload. Some restaurants take on the color of their context in this way; but others take on the color of their content. In Hong Kong, BIBO →P.164 was designed to look unfinished, so that it could be completed by the artwork its owners plan to cycle periodically through the space.

DRAMATIC spaces are not beholden to a single definition of luxury or allure; they come in a great variety of charismatic characters. Like graphic spaces, we will always seek out glamorous spaces for which we need to "dress up" and abide by certain codes to enter. They make us feel accepted or superior, and rewarded; we engage with their lack of banality. They rely on contrasts between innovation and tradition or scale and proportion, and on unexpected juxtapositions of objects and ideas: the banal touched by the beatific.

The extravagant scale of CARPE DIEM →P.222, for example, gives charisma to humble materials like rattan

THE PRESS CLUB →P.202
Melbourne (VIC), Australia

and carved wood. A round seat on the main floor ascends through the ceiling sensuously, to open, chrysalis-like, into a circular bar on the floor above.

Lee Broom's OLD TOM & ENGLISH →P.248 is an updated speakeasy mixed with a Victorian gentleman's club. It is a cocktail of the illicit and the elite, tropes

that have long been glamor's staple ingredients. Broom anchors the intimate, living room-like spaces with bold forms and then underscores their swanky neutrality with starlet-scarlet floors.

Sometimes these spaces exploit the high-tech; at other times, the low. Technology allows designers to invent new skins for spaces, playing with optics and texture in awe-inspiring ways. Low-tech approaches, however, can also make a space feel larger-than-life. In THE PRESS CLUB →P.202, March Studio dials up scale and uses fewer finishes that, nonetheless, have perfect tonal sympathy: beige leather upholstery, light wood, and, overhead, perforated brass modules. Somewhere between ceiling and floor, March has dovetailed the cool rational with the voluptuous and sublime.

* * *

Truly, today, we have been stuffed with the unblemished high-tech and the blandly mass-made. Now we're looking for the flawed, the man-handled, and the (mostly) authentic. Under a constant crush of information that makes us feel passive, we are looking for our own agency and accountability and, in this search, are turning to makers and curators, chefs and sommeliers, architects and interior designers. Before we consume anything at all, we want to know what it is that we are consuming. And then we want to be consumed by it.

OLD TOM & ENGLISH →P.248
London, United Kingdom

MONSIEUR BLEU →P.18 Paris, France

8

UNDERSTATEMENT

TEXT: SHONQUIS MORENO

To create elegant, understated interiors, designers measure them out in seemingly effortless doses. They diffuse the heavy aura of glamor, smooth out the rustic, and render the industrial space supple. Designers are co-opting certain elements of the old-fashioned, which they pare down, and the minimal, which they warm up. Their subtlety makes these eateries easier on the eyes and easy to digest, and if they have been simplified, they are by no means simplistic. Although temperamentally mild spaces tend to compete with neither the conversation nor the cookery, designers aren't making understated environments simply to suit the tastes of the broadest audience. Most often they represent creative approaches that frame and buoy the craftsmanship behind the scenes (and the scenery) in the kitchen. As in the kitchen, the ingredients of these interiors are meticulously selected, as a lack of garnishes, so to speak, leaves the designer little room for error in concealing missteps. If these measured interiors are more casually charismatic, they're not casually creative. THE GORGEOUS KITCHEN→P.10 by Blacksheep is a triumph of high-quality calm in the stress- and fast food–fueled fens of Heathrow Airport. The space is broadly open to passersby and is unlike the typical airport eatery with its high-traffic exhaustion of finishes and fare. Instead it retains the classy conviviality of a bistro's looks and menu. Without any flourishes that would diminish its comfort or give it airs, it is elegantly dressed in smoked glass, wood-paneled walls, and brass globe lights. Et voila. MARKET LANE COFFEE→P.32 by Hearth Studio is located in a historical, iconic building and is stylistically old-fashioned itself, but without pressing the point too far. There are no carved curlicues and no frilly finials to be found among the joinery, wood panels, and marble countertops. It is this simplicity that tells customers that the brand is going back to basics, that it is serious about quality. The ARCADE BAKERY→P.34 has an old-fashioned spirit, too, but it is intended to both match and contrast with the early-twentieth-century building whose lobby it inhabits so unobtrusively. ARCADE isn't a stand-alone space; instead it is a series of insertions into the existing polished granite walls. The bakery itself is tucked into a small room, its windows rimmed with wood paneling and simple bulb lights; a foldable awning marks the sales window. The tables also fold down from the walls, Murphy bed–style, and fold up again after business hours. By using hardwood mahogany and mahogany plywood, the designers suited the minimal design to the historical era the building memorializes, while also dedicating it to a contemporary moment when quality is cool again.

THEIR SUBTLETY MAKES THESE EATERIES EASIER ON THE EYES AND EASY TO DIGEST, AND IF THEY HAVE BEEN SIMPLIFIED, THEY ARE BY NO MEANS SIMPLISTIC

VERANDAH'S→P.12 minimalism would have had the unadorned, Kvadrat-upholstered, blond-wood ease of a Scandinavian interior, but GamFratesi interleaved its Nordic purity with vintage Indian furnishings and fixtures. This makes the space, like the fusion kitchen it serves, assume its own brand of refinement and nuance. If it were the chef, this interior would make a feast of very few flavors. NOPA→P.26, by Autoban, has more texture, but is just as tony. The surfaces and seating in this restaurant and bar recall the walnut-paneled interior of a mid-century sports car, and with this cool chic, the space responds to two urban exigencies at once. Situated in an elegant corner of green space–deprived Istanbul, it boasts vertical green walls and a waterfall that splashes beneath a ceiling of retractable skylights. It also exemplifies the softspoken but swank space that provides counterpoint to today's rustic and industrial chic. At a quick glance, HER MAJESTY'S PLEASURE→P.42 by +tongtong looks almost generically contemporary, but in actuality it is a quiet patchwork of references. It makes allusions to Adirondack chairs and 1950s summer cabins, and to soda fountains with their white, marble-topped bars and checkered flooring. These are punctuated with tufted club chair bar stools and gleaming copper seating. The rest of the space is pared down to a featherweight economy with skeleton shelving and a plywood bar whose structure is exposed but sheltered under a clear gloss. Readers be warned: understated has never meant underbuilt. Just because an interior is soft-spoken doesn't mean it isn't full of conviction.

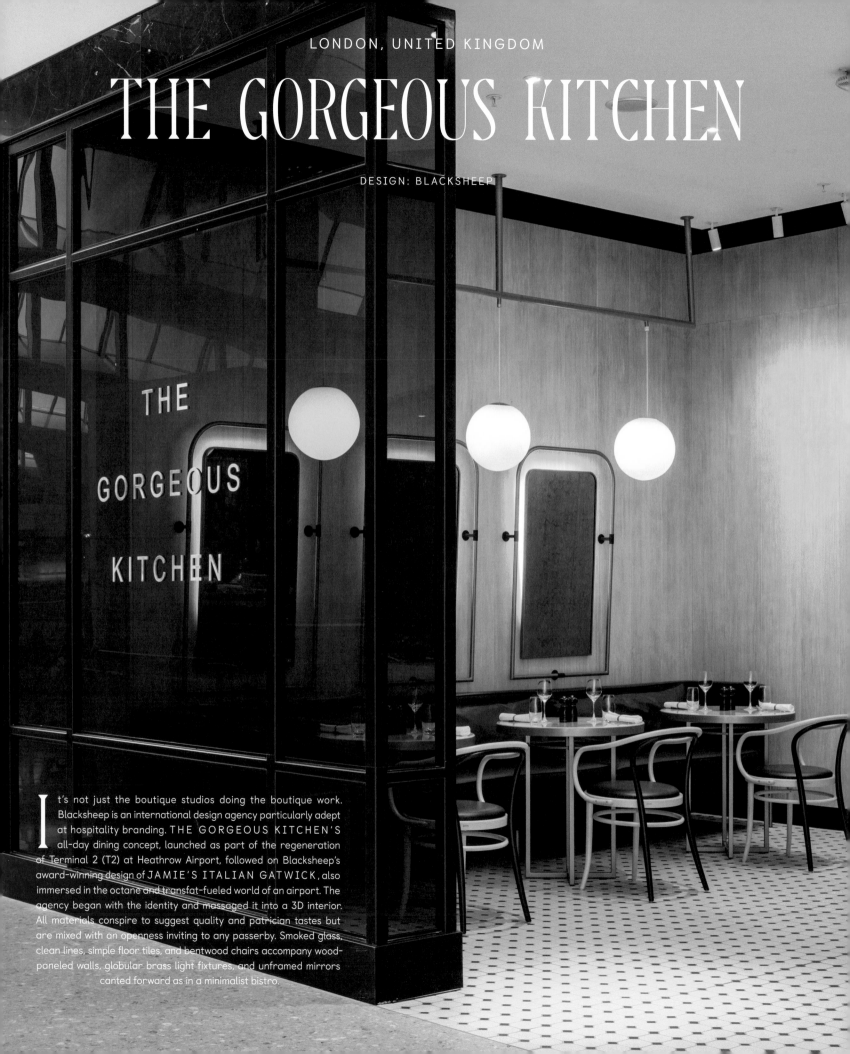

THE GORGEOUS KITCHEN

DESIGN: BLACKSHEEP

THE
GORGEOUS
KITCHEN

I t's not just the boutique studios doing the boutique work. Blacksheep is an international design agency particularly adept at hospitality branding. THE GORGEOUS KITCHEN'S all-day dining concept, launched as part of the regeneration of Terminal 2 (T2) at Heathrow Airport, followed on Blacksheep's award-winning design of JAMIE'S ITALIAN GATWICK, also immersed in the octane and transfat-fueled world of an airport. The agency began with the identity and massaged it into a 3D interior. All materials conspire to suggest quality and patrician tastes but are mixed with an openness inviting to any passerby. Smoked glass, clean lines, simple floor tiles, and bentwood chairs accompany wood-paneled walls, globular brass light fixtures, and unframed mirrors canted forward as in a minimalist bistro.

COPENHAGEN, DENMARK

VERANDAH

DESIGN: GAMFRATESI

NORDIC FURNITURE AND VINTAGE INDIAN ELEMENTS COEXIST, ALONGSIDE A BLURRING OF INDOOR AND OUTDOOR

I conoclasts are those who have studied the icons deeply enough to explode them. For Italian furniture label GamFratesi's design of this Nordic-Indian fusion restaurant, housed inside the 1930s Standard Building, the design team combined history and renewal to reflect the chef's experimental approach to materials and techniques. Stine Gam and Enrico Fratesi started at this cross-cultural, cross-temporal intersection and created furniture that reflects tradition, but with a minimalist's brush. They used a materials palette of blond wood, brass, and delicately hued Kvadrat textiles. Nordic furniture and vintage Indian elements coexist, alongside a blurring of indoor and outdoor, achieved by constructing a shallow podium that evokes, yes, that interstitial architectural element—the veranda.

MONSIEUR BLEU

DESIGN: JOSEPH DIRAND ARCHITECTURE

D irand played with the tension between classical forms of architecture and more whimsical elements, using illusion as the motif of this brasserie interior. As is his usual practice, Dirand simultaneously responded to his site while amplifying its character. He exploited the topography of the floor-slab, using it as a guide to insert a discrete space and function into the existing building, which was monumental, heavy, and bleakly grand. Before he began to design, Dirand imagined MONSIEUR BLEU as a man of particular character and allied this character with that of the space: a nineteenth-century sophisticate—"a dandy, a poet, an architect, or an engineer"—with a meticulously manicured beard.

PARIS, FRANCE

LE FLANDRIN

DESIGN: JOSEPH DIRAND ARCHITECTURE

With a little sleight of hand, Dirand makes the mezzanines vanish and rashes of pink brick and limestone re-surface in this classy classic brasserie. Guests enter LE FLANDRIN through a heroic archway, only to be greeted with the intimate illumination of suspended glass lamps. He used smoked mirrors reflected in mirrors to amplify the shifts of light that take place over the course of a day. Green marble, natural wood, and mohair velvet upholstery give only the gentlest suggestion of decadence. Dirand designed the lounge to pay homage to Czech Cubism, with black lacquer gilt trim wood panelling and Calcutta Gold marble. The space's concentric orga-nization maintains a sense of privacy while offering interesting sightlines from all angles.

CAFÉ ARTSCIENCE

DESIGN: MATHIEU LEHANNEUR

Many of Mathieu Lehanneur's designs are about purifying and self-soothing in a world at the mercy of the senses, one in which we must reconcile the low-tech and the high, the left brain and the right. With longtime collaborator, American scientist David Edwards, Lehanneur outfitted CAFÉ ARTSCIENCE as an auditorium, bar, concept shop, and art gallery, calling it "the missing link between scientific laboratory and literary café." In the open-plan space it is furnishings like the voluptuous white cement bar and an undulating green velvet sofa that guide circulation and suggest the function of space. Private dinners and workshops are held in the Honeycomb, clad with hex-shaped slate tiles to represent the intelligence of the hive mind of bees.

ISTANBUL, TURKEY

NOPA

DESIGN: AUTOBAN

NOPA fuses architecture, interior, and product design with some seriously lush landscaping—and a retractable glass ceiling in the back. Local design office Autoban created bespoke lighting and furniture for the space while borrowing colors, materials, and textures from nature. They selected the stone flooring for its varying tones, which form a continuous geometric pattern throughout. At the rear, the soundtrack, so to speak, for the open-air dining room is composed by an actual waterfall and the velvety green walls of a vertical garden. The bar, which runs the length of the interior and then slips outdoors to coil into an island, is NOPA'S focal point and recalls the new leather interior of a classic convertible with the top down.

BANGKOK, THAILAND

SALA RATTANAKOSIN EATERY AND BAR

DESIGN: ONION

While transforming retail into resort space, Siriyot Chaiamnuay and Arisara Chaktranon of Bangkok-based Onion staged this restaurant and bar to feel aged as well as it was renewed. Framing otherworldly views of temples, waterfronts, and sunsets over the historical city was the focus of Onion's design. They opted for laminated glass, partly reflective and partly transparent, in which the scenery and its reflections can be observed at the same time. They also unearthed the most remarkable architectural details: ornamented balcony handrails and the original brick hidden behind crumbling cement walls. Onion also inserted new materials to flesh out S A L A R A T T A N A K O S I N' S contemporary character including dark-gold laminated glass, black and white ceramic tiles, and aluminum panels.

MARKET LANE COFFEE

DESIGN: HEARTH

This coffee shop stands in an expansive and well-glazed corner stall in an early twentieth-century heritage building in the Queen Victoria Market. The interior, by Melbourne-based Sarah Trotter of local studio Hearth, takes its cues from the building's original facade and tiled interior, however, Trotter also introduced new materials. American Oak timber and a black 2pac finish generate texture and ensure that some elements pop for the eye while others recede. She also incorporated vintage apron hooks, an old wash sink, and an equipment display in a vintage chemist's cabinet. By keeping the main joinery elements off the walls, she kept original sightlines open, a rare element in a market stall, which is typically divvied up and obscured with storage space.

ARCADE BAKERY

DESIGN: WORKSTEAD

Inspired by the existing forms and materials—vaulted ceilings, stone, and terrazzo—but also in contrast to them, Stefanie Brechbuehler and Robert Highsmith describe their design of the ARCADE BAKERY as "interventionist." They have completed a series of small-scale interventions in the existing little-used lobby at the foot of TriBeCa's Merchants Square Building, built in the early 1900s. The augmented lobby became a bakery lined seamlessly with seating nooks, display areas, a cold-prep area, and a retail alcove. When the bakery is open, these elements fold out of the walls to form tables and a canopy over the retail counter. By using hardwood mahogany and mahogany plywood, the duo underscored the venerable age of the building but in a crisp, clean way that suits both eras.

PEG + PATRIOT

DESIGN: ARIANA REES ROBERTS

They just don't make it like that anymore is a saying that does not apply to PEG + PATRIOT. This bar, set in the Town Hall Hotel, serves spirits, vermouth, and liqueurs that are either produced in-house and on-site or sourced from labels that believe in carefully crafting their product. On the menu are original, refined beverages that don't take themselves too seriously: nectars like Sumac My Bitch Up use distilled Greek yogurt gin, and Pho Money Pho Problems is made from Vietnamese aromatic infused vodka. The interior reflects this once old-fashioned, but now contemporary attitude in its simple, honest materials—marble, wood, brass, old parquet flooring, a dark and neutral palette, and straightforward, unfussy details.

BRONDA

DESIGN: FUTUDESIGN

Futudesign concocted this modern brasserie in the center of the city by slicing it into three zones. At the front, a cocktail bar is separated from the dining room by a glass-walled, walk-in, custom-made wine cabinet that keeps sightlines and light-lines open between the two. In the rear, a convertible space can be partitioned into four smaller nooks or opened completely to become an extension of the dining hall. Futu created bespoke sofas and tables, and otherwise drew from a simple materials palette of oak, brass, marble, leather, and glass. The bar floor is tiled in a pattern inspired by a Helsinki sea chart, and large window apertures create an engaging play between diners and the city's streets.

HER MAJESTY'S PLEASURE

DESIGN: +TONGTONG

Toronto-based John Tong and Kateryna Nebesna created this cheerful, multitasking space with its coquettish name, where clients get manicures, pedicures, and blowouts. HER MAJESTY'S PLEASURE contains multiple spaces within one, including a café, retail boutique, beauty salon, and bar. The café and bar area, simultaneously luxe and pared-down, includes a white marble bar and a row of folded copper stools. The makeup lounge becomes distinct from the rest of the interior by taking the form of a wood cabin; meanwhile, the pedicure zone is demarcated by a long, raised wooden deck lined with Muskoka chairs to recall a verandah. Guests sit at the marble bar as they get their hair done, while bartenders serve lowballs and organic juice.

MODERN MUSINGS

TEXT: SHONQUIS MORENO

Nothing too much, and Know thyself. Socrates's maxims recommending candor and moderation are a good starting point when talking about minimal modernist spaces and Scandinavian-inflected design. Instead of relying on details and ornament, the projects in this chapter use minimal materials and color schemes wisely, making statements through juxtapositions, contrasts, repetition, and even empty space. Their look and feel originate in their function and remain unembellished. Simplicity and clarity of form is privileged; superfluous details are eliminated. The designer's or architect's emphasis on being forthright, paring away, and respecting craftsmanship and materials reflects the philosophy of the chef in the kitchen, who is also striving to unite aesthetics and function while respecting the handmaking and the ingredients.

The JURY CAFE→P.52 by Biasol: Design Studio, with its carpenterly and monolithically plywood interior, is lacquered into smoothness, but with a clear finish that underscores the Modernist penchant for truth to materials. Here, the materials toolkit consists of plywood and oak, bare (energy-saving) bulbs, and paint. The triangular coffered walls and counter make the architecture the skin, the revelation of structure and materials being favored over concealment or alteration, which are seen as disingenuous. What you see is what you should get. And with just a few particular small sections of the wall painted black, white, or pink, this exposure of the structure is only emphasized. In contrasting pattern of triangles, consisting of beams repeated at 45-degree angles instead of the usual 90, Biasol put a contemporary spin on good old orthogonal modernism.

Simple contrast, in deliberate doses, figures largely in the projects on the following pages. The MIKKELER BAR→P.74 consists of an all-white room with seating and an adjoining bar room tiled in glossy black. Tiles are common to many a minimalist eatery: aside from looking clean of line, they're easy to clean. Contrast is also created through the variety of seating and lighting selected by Femmes Régionales. There is only one of each type in the room, each with an unconventional form whose quirkiness suggests an individual personality. This motley crew of character-furnishings, then, gives the distinct impression that the pieces are engaged in (silent, but lively) conversation with each other. In this sense, a limited range of objects and materials adds up to more than the sum of their parts. Using a single material or a few materials monolithically doesn't mean resigning oneself to uniformity; the projects in this chapter demonstrate that the rhythm this produces may be orderly but never feels dull. In London's

THE PROJECTS IN THIS CHAPTER USE MINIMAL MATERIALS AND COLOR SCHEMES WISELY, MAKING STATEMENTS THROUGH JUXTAPOSITIONS, CONTRASTS, REPETITION, AND EVEN EMPTY SPACE

OPSO→P.48, Athens-based K-Studio cleverly threads a single element through the space to unite its different floor levels and functions. A black steel framework morphs from counter bar to shelving to storage cabinets, from refrigerators and to waitstaff service stations.

In GAMSEI→P.50, the repetition of a few organic materials—wooden shelves and walls, ceramic bottles, a ceiling grid from which the bottles are hung—makes the space graphical. Meanwhile the bareness and clarity of all surfaces showcase the craftsmanship that is an expression of both the mission and the menu of the restaurant.

FARMSHOP MARIN→P.78 in the Bay Area is a restaurant by Commune that just wants to be itself—not a French bistro, not an Italian trattoria, but a place to eat laid-back, lean, clean California cuisine. The truth-to-ingredients practiced by the kitchen is paralleled in the plain luxury of the design materials and organization: macrame lamp cords, mid-century modern wooden furnishings, and artist-crafted objects and art, including a black-and-white photo-mural of a corn field in which diners on two sides of the main dining room are immersed. It is both textural and locational; this is where your food comes from.

Walking into fashion designer Henrik Vibskov's DEN PLETTEDE GRIS→P.54 café in Copenhagen is like walking into a room-size loom. At first glance, it might appear complex, but the materials kit is simple: paint in six colors, repeated in stripes of varying thickness, black elastic bands, and oak dowels. Through a few well-chosen ingredients—though it contains no textiles—the deeply textural interior becomes a textile itself, evoking coziness precisely through its minimalism.

OPSO

DESIGN: K-STUDIO

Greek inspired and London made, this eatery is organized by a central spine that runs the length of the 186-square-meter interior from a coffee bar at the entrance to a common table in the rear, establishing two zones and a change of levels. The open-plan space is organized via an extensive, slender steel framework that forms an open storage system containing waiter's stations, wine fridges, and food cabinets, as well as wooden shelves and potted plants. A brass rail under the ceiling tidily conceals lighting fixtures. The Athens-based design team combined bespoke furnishings with natural materials found in old Athenian cafés. They wed oak panels, leather upholstery, and brass accents with hand-laid Terrazzo flooring and Kavala marble wall cladding and table tops.

MUNICH, GERMANY

GAMSEI

DESIGN: BUERO WAGNER

In GAMSEI, the saying "think global, act local" becomes think local, act local. Food and cocktail ingredients come from local farmers. Even designers Wagner and Kreft are Munich locals. The two drew this concept into the interior, using oak from the area and artisanal ceramics, relying on collaboration with local craftsmen in step with the restaurant's larger business goals. Repetition of simple items like ceramic jars gives both clarity and rich texture to the space. Among wooden surfaces and concrete floors, the jars stand in phalanxes on shelves and hang in clusters from the ceiling. The designers also worked to remove barriers, literal and figurative, by storing ingredients in plain sight and by inserting two facing amphitheater-style benches that remove the counter between barkeep and guest.

MELBOURNE (VIC),
AUSTRALIA

JURY CAFE

DESIGN: BIASOL: DESIGN STUDIO

Biasol believes in design's power to convey and elicit emotion. Their JURY CAFE is collared by the bluestone walls of a Melbourne historical site, a former prison, decommissioned less than 20 years ago. The designers took the notion of irreverence as their conceptual starting point with a twofold goal: they wanted to respect the site's dark history, while giving it a second, brighter life. This motif was used literally: the dark bluestone walls contrast with a fresh scheme of vivid colors and blond wood. Raw materials like plywood, structural timbers, and concrete establish a geometric pattern that tattoos the café's feature wall. Biasol's scheme preserves some of the character of the original building while making it part of something larger and more luminous.

COPENHAGEN, DENMARK

DEN PLETTEDE GRIS

DESIGN: HENRIK VIBSKOV

T he atelier of fashion designer Henrik Vibskov
shares a house with this tiny coffeeshop called
THE DOTTED PIG on Paper Island in the
Christianshavn district of Copenhagen. Vibskov was
trying to create the feeling of being inside a piano when he
dressed the 14-square-meter interior with textiles and
elastics in six different colors to form piano-like strings
along the walls. The topmost section of each wall in the
room is striped with wooden dowels that extend from the
wall and over which Vibskov has stretched black elastic
bands. The effect is of a woven textile that, in criss-cross-
ing, casts a thicket of slender shadows. Under this textile
piano, the walls are painted in colorful stripes. Red and
pink at the top, they descend into a charcoal and rust-
colored dado, and create a cheerfully melodic theme
when taken altogether.

54

MIKKELLER & FRIENDS

DESIGN: RUM4

This bar stands in stark contrast to the dark messy pub of yore. This local microbrewer's collaborations with designers and craftspeople—making everything from bottle labels and interiors to gluten-free recipes—continues with Karsten K. Lülloff and Kristian Lillelund of Rum4. They concocted this modern bierstube of raw materials to create a masculine but cheerful feel. Hard edges, straight lines, and stout wood mingle with glossy turquoise floors, bright blond surfaces, custom picnic benches, tables, and lamps. They carved out a variety of standing and sitting spaces in order to allow guests to establish personal space without feeling isolated. This is where Copenhagen beer aficionados will want to be during Danish winters.

STOCKHOLM, SWEDEN

FINEFOOD KÄRLEK OCH MAT

DESIGN: NOTE

Note uses colorful minimalism to seamlessly transition from day into evening at this eatery, which shifts from café to lunch destination and then to bistro as night falls. The space is located in Hammarby Sjöstad, an emerging district in the city's south where the government has imposed strict environmental standards. The designers drew from Jordan Sullivan's photographic series of America's mist-shrouded Death Valley to create their color and materials palettes. They rendered the subtle variations in stone and sky and captured soft shifts of light that transmute harsh terrain into poetic landscape; striated chevrons, and pastel furnishings give the space a gentle glow amid the harder seams of graphical floors and walls.

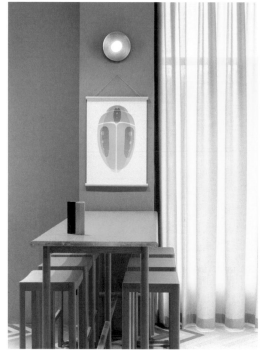

THE SPRINGS

DESIGN: DESIGN, BITCHES

As the studio name suggests, and under the influence of LA's cultural fusions and undersung architectural experimentation, Catherine Johnson and Rebecca Rudolph, who are Design, Bitches, think design should be expressive and pop. They describe THE SPRINGS, a campus comprising a raw vegan restaurant, yoga studio, and wine and organic juice bars, as "relentlessly optimistic" and "a crisp, bright pause amidst the industrial exhaust." Apt, considering this wellness oasis is situated in a 1980s concrete block warehouse between the Arts District and a boulevard that rumbles under heavy trucking. Because THE SPRINGS is about sparking transformation—physical, philosophical, locational—it is equipped with planters, a warm, laid-back palette, and skylights that drench the interior in natural light.

A CRISP,
BRIGHT PAUSE
AMIDST THE
INDUSTRIAL
EXHAUST

OSLO, NORWAY

VINO VERITAS ECO-GASTROBAR

DESIGN: MASQUESPACIO

Valencia, Spain-based Masquespacio is directed by Ana Milena Hernández Palacios. VINO VERITAS hails from the Andalusian region La Alpujarra and is Oslo's introduction to ecological Spanish gastronomy. Palacios started by making the space familiar to Scandinavians, using white-washed wooden walls and ceilings and a solid oak floor. Then, to reflect the menu, she brought in Spanish culture with old Andalusian balcony rail-ings, baskets, grass esparto blinds, and Spanish clay tiles. She highlighted traditional craftsman-ship by featuring elements like handmade raffia, esparto and cord lamps, caning mounted to the walls, solid wood tables, and textiles Palacios herself designed. To finish, she lined the space with green plants and turquoise upholstery to infuse it with the color of life.

HELSINKI, FINLAND

STORY

DESIGN: JOANNA LAAJISTO CREATIVE STUDIO

THIS EASY-GOING EATERY SERVES UP A HELPING OF MODERNITY WATERED WITH SMALL-BATCH WINES

Joanna Laajisto's S T O R Y provides an anchoring narrative for the rehabilitated Old Market Hall, a cultural heritage site from 1889. Situated at its high-ceilinged heart, this easy-going eatery serves up a helping of modernity watered with small-batch wines. Laajisto wanted guests to consider it a destination even though it is a transit area splintered into three sections by walkways. Laajisto used oak, leather, and stone, and tapped local wood artisan Tebian to handcraft the tables. In response to heritage constraints—she couldn't hang lamps from the 10-meter ceiling—Laajisto hit on custom-made solutions like her intimate Edit2 lamp and wire fish traps found in a local summer cottage that she turned into rustic maritime lighting fixtures.

MIKKELLER BAR VIKTORIAGADE

DESIGN: FEMMES RÉGIONALES

MIKKELLER is the DeBeers of beer bars: the brand recruits designers to match the quality of their microbrews in anything from bottle labels to interiors. Caroline Hansen and Mie Nielsen took their cues from the brewer's innovations on ages-old crafting techniques and, after a pubcrawl of their own (research), updated the look of the typical old Danish pub by mashing up modern furnishings and fixtures. Around wooden tables and benches, a chunky plywood armchair faces high blond stools, standing legs akimbo, and a yellow Mecanoo chair sitting beside a black Thonet. As if mirroring the interactions of their future users, these odd companions appear to be engaged in lively but silent conversation. You can almost imagine one of them saying, "So a guy walks into a bar …"

DISCO VOLANTE

DESIGN: MADAME MOHR

The five-year-old Madame Mohr creative collective likes to explore "ethics and aesthetics in all scales." Since they offer design services in parametrics, feasibility studies, and prototyping, the minimalist, 1970s- and 1980s-inflected DISCO VOLANTE restaurant represents the lighter side of the studio's portfolio. Disco, its name alluding to the ship of a James Bond villain but also simply meaning "flying disc," is a southern Italian pizzeria that opened on the pie-cutting edge of the Viennese pizza trend. Amidst white surfaces and wooden chairs, the wood-fired oven becomes the focal point, disguised as a giant disco ball glittering with 7,500 mirror tiles. And, as disco balls are wont to do, it rotates at—not quite a disco beat—a single revolution per minute.

LARKSPUR (CA), UNITED STATES

FARMSHOP MARIN

DESIGN: COMMUNE DESIGN

For this locally grown, farm-to-table, artisanal restaurant, Commune created an interior exuding laid-back luxury. The owners wanted FARMSHOP to be itself—not a French bistro, not an Italian trattoria, but a Californian food space born and bred. They made it Californian by asking local artisans to make everything inside. Sculptor Alma Allen made tables and bar tops from black walnut and hand-forged metal. Robert Lewis transformed macramé lights into Adolf Loos–inspired chandeliers while ceramicist Adam Silverman furnished hurricane lamps and candleholders and Heath made the tiles. Bolinas craftsman Trip Carpenter and LA's Michael Boyd did the furniture. Across two walls, surveying the room serenely, is a mural photographed by local Pirkle Jones.

RAMONA

DESIGN: MM18 ARQUITETURA

RAMONA is a restaurant and bar that inhabits three floors of a famous city corner, including the basement, ground floor, and mezzanine. The interior design surfaced from the previously existing structure, which was carefully preserved and protected whenever possible. The coffered ceiling nearly mirrors the stone floor while both are mirrored in a wall of beveled, brick-shaped, reflective tiles that pull light through the narrow, windowless space, hide the restrooms, and provide a shiny but slightly rough texture beside the glossily lacquered and bookmatched ironwood wall panels. In RAMONA, MM18 has invoked a refined, midcentury modern spirit while using a contemporary language.

GDYNIA, POLAND

ALTHAUS

DESIGN: PB/STUDIO

This traditional Bavarian restaurant looks more nationally neutral than its menu, but the modern interior has great clarity and calm. A large glazed facade allows passersby to gaze hungrily in on a minimal but domestic scene and a limited color and materials palette. Kozarski featured golden oak, bottle green, and copper in the lamps, mosaics, and the chandelier, alluding to traditional Bavarian beer production methods. Each room offers a different flavor: calfskin and whitewashed wood are paired on the street level while, on the upper floor, the bar and a buffet are paneled in dark green. These elements come together in the rooms surrounding the bar: green reappears in velvet upholstery and oak, white brick, and classic Thonet chairs bespeak the comfort of one's own kitchen.

RADEGAST BEER PUB

DESIGN: IO STUDIO

Radegast may not have actually been a god of fertility, hospitality, and ... beer worshipped by Western Slavs, but the name means, roughly, dear guest, and is as forthright and inviting as the interior of this beer pub. While emphasizing the beauty of craftsmanship, the interior is a wholly modern rendition of traditional technology, materials, and coziness. Lozenge-shaped tables and other oak furniture are paired with two-tone classic bentwood Thonet chairs. The rounded ceiling and walls are gridded with blue lines inspired by Czech porcelain and paired with light gray oak wall panels and black steel and copper details. Staggered oak baulks and irregular diagonals interrupt the "tiles," a strongly graphical element that leaves enough blank space to let the ornament breathe.

SAUL ZONA 14

DESIGN: TALLER KEN

SAUL ZONA 14 is a colorful synthesis of fashion, design, art, objects, and food that brings culture and commerce together. The facade takes its cues from Guatemala City's legacy architecture, particularly the deep ornamental window niches of Spanish colonial buildings. The building's exterior is clad with molded fiberglass panels finished in smooth plaster stucco that looks as if it has been stretched taut. The restrooms are tattooed with geometric tiles and mirror while the long terrace boasts an unusual textile canopy. Fashioned from 1,000 pounds of thread that hang from a steel structure in a palette of deep green, teal, yellow, and black, it invokes the lush verdure of the country.

PIZZA WITH NO NAME →P.122 Reykjavík, Iceland

ROUGH & LOCAL

TEXT: SHONQUIS MORENO

Today, we are squeezed between the flawless high-tech and the bland, uniformly mass-made, between plastic and its pollution. In response, we're looking for authenticity and accountability. To create everything from our spaces and belongings to our food, we're looking for craftsmen and curators, makers and synthesizers, who can show us how to live with fewer things of greater value. With the prevalence of do-it-yourself, seasonal, regional, farm-to-table, nose-to-tail eating, and craft drinking, distilling and brewing, we're not just looking for stage sets and branded experiences, but masterfully made expressions of what we believe in.

At either end of the spectrum, the rustic and industrial aesthetics may seem carpenterly and casual, mechanical and muscular, but they are both about concern for the well-made. The eating spaces in this chapter are forthright. Sometimes they're designed by the business owners themselves. They may rely on their context and their approach to the food to guide the creation of the space. They may look to the future by honoring the past, that indefinable past that we are talking about when we say, they just don't make it like that anymore.

The SALUMERIA LAMURI→P.96 charcuterie stands in a 100-year-old butcher shop. It was shaped not just by excavating the original space from beneath the cheap accretions of decades, but by strategically inserting contemporary materials and furnishings that serve to frame and broadcast the original elements of the space.

The maritime-rustic character of the HOG ISLAND OYSTER FARM→P.106 reflects the fact that it is a working oyster farm that also sells fresh, wholesome food. The indoor and outdoor spaces have grown organically over the years, a work-in-progress that looks utterly native to its place. Its furnishings signal the sea: a sun-bleached ship's wheel, a pair of Cape Cod chairs, a worn fishing boat. From its hull, staff sell artisanal local breads and cheeses, but mostly oysters and other seafood fresh from the catch, to be eaten at picnic benches beside the bay that are equipped with shucking tools.

GLASSERIE→P.116 is coastal too, but not rural. This restaurant, in an 1860s glass fixture factory that also housed its workers, sits on the lip of Greenpoint, Brooklyn. Here, owner Sara Conklin designed the interiors to be as true to place as her chef is true to ingredients in the kitchen. She exposed the old brick, found wooden benches and original factory subflooring and even used light fixtures representative of the

WE'RE LOOKING FOR CRAFTSMEN AND CURATORS, MAKERS AND SYNTHESIZERS, WHO CAN SHOW US HOW TO LIVE WITH FEWER THINGS OF GREATER VALUE

products made on-site long ago. Glasserie assumes no airs but its deftly crafted, high-quality food suits its authentic interiors just-so.

The SMOKESTACK AT MAGNOLIA BREWERY→P.108 also features a historical factory aesthetic, thanks to Nothing Something. The designers used antiques and architectural salvage to give it an old-fashioned saloon-rustic look that reflects the fact that the owners brew their beer on the premises. Its double-height volume and many-paned interior factory windows are accompanied by wood paneling, wood-plank floors, and wooden benches. It is a carpenterly sensibility that is taken a degree further in the precise penny-tiling and detailed, decorative joinery of the saloon-rustic bar ALAMEDA→P.102 in Brooklyn, designed by the long-haired, bearded brothers who are hOmE Studio. Rustic and industrial, when associated with art, can assume an aura of glamor in spite of roughness.

On the other extreme, HAWKSMOOR SPITALFIELD'S→P.126 by Macaulay Sinclair and Huw Gott has an urban glamor, but it is essentially a factory-rustic grotto that could once have served as a subway platform. Blue tile and copper surfaces line the intimately vaulted basement space under a low black ceiling. Commune didn't try to deny that this was once a strip club; the designers preserved a sense of the space's maturity by salvaging materials from local historical buildings, including tinted mirrors, glazed bricks, a brass wall made from old elevator doors, and wooden tables that once stood in a chemistry lab.

In every meal that is handmade, and in every draft that is tapped or brewed by hand, we are looking for morsels of something real when we go out. We choose and broadcast our values by seeking out the purest ingredients, literally and metaphorically, in what we do, what we own, and in how and where we eat.

NEW YORK (NY), UNITED STATES

NAVY

DESIGN: JEANETTE DALROT,
AKIVA ELSTEIN
AND MATTHEW ABRAMCYK

With the culinary focus on seafood and vegetables, this 51-seat bar and restaurant has a maritime Second World War sensibility and is a follow-up to the rough elegance of SMITH & MILLS in TriBeCa. Its interior features a whitewashed floor, counters tiled with abstracted sailboat patterns, and old wooden school chairs. Wine storage consists of old leather straps ranged together along the rear wall. Red and white semaphore flags serve as partitions, Japanese indigo textiles become curtains, and French linen and vintage military canvas dress the walls. Even the waitstaff and bartenders are dressed in bespoke vintage work jackets and elegant frocks by Lady & Butler.

SALUMERIA LAMURI

DESIGN: WIBKE ISENBERG-COHEN

L AMURI explores the authenticity and tropes of the rustic, old-fashioned Italian salumeria. This charcuterie and luncheonette in Kreuzberg is located in a restored butcher shop dating to 1870. The space doesn't just look the part, it sells quality Italian products—wines, pasta, pestos, marmalades, and sweets homemade from vintage Italian recipes or imported from Italy. Also on offer: a daily lunch menu of light fare. The designer chose multiple patterns of hand-painted tiles to dress the walls and floors, and original oil paintings to clad the high ornate ceilings; customers will feel as if they have walked into a traditional Italian delicacy shop with a history and interior that reaches back for generations.

FLEISCHEREI

DESIGN: THEZIMMER

Rough and cozy, old and new, this century-old butcher shop has become a bar. Michael Grzesiak and Sebastian Stiess tailored made-to-measure wooden inserts to underscore the shape of the existing trapezoidal space. While preserving a sense of the interior's age, the designers also wanted to create a contemporary space that would feel comfortable in its own skin. The ornate existing space featured original Villeroy & Boch ceramic tiles and a reverse-painted glass ceiling. The two inserted a massive oak-tiled bar with chunky offset cubes, creating texture and anchoring a geometric theme. The warmth of oiled wooden surfaces—oak bar, pear flooring—relieves the chillier atmosphere of the former butchery and as it ages, it will also begin to tell a story about the passage of time through space.

ALAMEDA

DESIGN: HOME

Masters of timber-and-tile chic, Evan and Oliver Haslegrave's interiors preserve the famed look and feel of the Brooklyn bar while giving it their own spin, replete with long beards, long hair, and bare feet. One reviewer praised the Greenpoint bar by calling it "small town," which is exactly what the big city cognoscenti are craving. The brothers carpentered their signature chevron pattern in woods of varying tones to create a striped patchwork across the wooden table-tops and across the white-tile walls. Crooked wooden stripes running from the front to the rear of the room draw the eyes inward, while penny tiles form a U-shaped pathway around the circular island bar. Crowning it all, chunky wooden ceiling lights, like farmland models of the Empire State Building, give the ceiling a lumber-jack Art Deco sensibility.

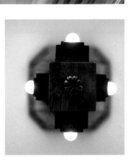

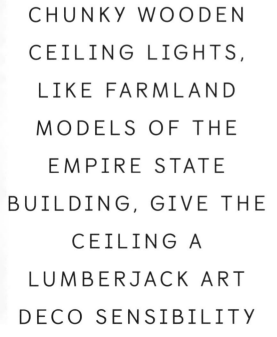

CHUNKY WOODEN CEILING LIGHTS, LIKE FARMLAND MODELS OF THE EMPIRE STATE BUILDING, GIVE THE CEILING A LUMBERJACK ART DECO SENSIBILITY

DOUGHNUT VAULT

DESIGN: BRENDAN SODIKOFF

C hef and designer Brendan Sodikoff bought an old bank vault. At the time, he was making some pretty posh doughnuts, so it seemed appropriate to sell them out of the vault. Now, because only about eight people can fit inside, locals line up down Franklin Street to deposit their money in return for a pumpkin softie with chestnut glaze or a peanut old fashioned with banana chips.

Methods as old as the doughnut itself are used to handcraft these confections in small batches. Sodikoff stripped the space back to its original brick and terracotta tile, and then added wood surfaces, cushy leather armchairs, an ornate nineteenth-century cash register, and a crystal chandelier. It's the details—with their mouths full—that speak of the halcyon days of hand-making.

DOUGHNUT VAULT

◆

BUTTERMILK
OLD FASHIONED...2.00

GINGERBREAD
STACK...........3.00

GLAZED (Chestnut,
Vanilla, Chocolate.)...3.00

Dollar Coffee
FRANÇOIS' FAVORITE. 1.

NOW OFFERING
Seasonal Jelly
Doughnuts

Enter

HOG ISLAND OYSTER FARM

DESIGN: TERRY SAWYER AND JOHN FINGER

This community-oriented eatery and working oyster farm has a rustic maritime look so descriptive it could simply replace the menu. Ornament is spare, but eloquent: a ship's wheel is so sun-bleached it might be driftwood, and a whitewashed clapboard house is guarded by Cape Cod chairs. The design of the spaces by co-founders Terry Sawyer and John Finger has evolved out of usage. At a carved Yule marble bar in the bow of an old wooden boat, staff sell shucked and barbequed oysters and local breads, cheeses, charcuterie, beer, and wine. Picnic tables sit at bay's edge, equipped with a grill, shucking tools, lemons, and hot sauce. At the front, The Hog Shack, a retail kiosk, is where freshly harvested shellfish are sold, alive and unshucked—as fresh as the Shack is deliciously aged.

SMOKESTACK AT MAGNOLIA BREWERY

DESIGN: NOTHING SOMETHING

The studio name seems apt. At SMOKESTACK, Nothing Something basically created history out of myriad constituent parts. Kevin Landwehr of the New York-based practice collaborated with designer Devin Becker to give this barbecue joint and microbrewery a delicious sense of age. Located in San Francisco's Dogpatch, a gentrifying post-industrial warehouse and emerging arts district, it follows the democratic rituals of beer gardens, Wild West saloons, and backyard BBQs the world over, welcoming guests at large communal tables or bentwood bar stools for bellying up. From custom metal shelving, black acacia wood tables, and old-fashioned bulbs to a brass panel tap unit and a quartzite bar top, the designers chose details meticulously to ensure the space looks as if it has been there long enough to generate a history of its own.

108

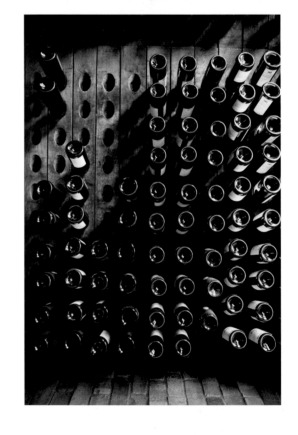

A SOCIOLOGICAL STUDY
IN CREATING INTERACTION
THROUGH SPACE

GJELINA

DESIGN: MARSHALL PROJECTS

S am Marshall describes his eatery on Abbot Kinney Boulevard in Venice as "inside-out"and "a sociological study in creating interaction through space." Intersecting communal tables fill the main dining room and en-circle a charcuterie bar, creating the circulation and organization of the restaurant. Marshall relied on finishes like brick and rough salvaged wood that are typically found on the outside of a building but which entirely define the interior of G J E L I N A . At the same time, sofas, floor lamps, and other furniture usually associated with interiors make the outdoor patio feel like an indoor room

NEW YORK (NY), UNITED STATES

THE BRESLIN

DESIGN: ROMAN AND WILLIAMS

This 150-seat restaurant provides counterpoint to the Ace Hotel in which it lives, and to the bright scenography of the oyster bar →P.176 by the same designers a few doors down. This space is dark, wooden, lived-in, and heavy—a saloon of the highest order, or as suggested by the wood paneling and the post-and-beam system, an English pub with uncharacteristically superb food. Fencing rescued from a Pacific Northwest ranch becomes flooring and contrasts with the custom-milled panels, booths, and columns that were glazed in glossy brown, green, and black oil paint. Essentially, the interior promises what the kitchen delivers: classic, working-class English fare—thoroughly refined.

LOS ANGELES (CA), UNITED STATES

L.A. CHAPTER

DESIGN: COMMUNE DESIGN

Commune wanted this brasserie to be made "by L.A. for L.A." Off the eclectically furnished Ace Hotel lobby, like the menu, its interior mixes fresh flavors with familiar recipes. Commune brought in 16 artists and artisans from California and Mexico to honor the history of the 1927 building, a former cinema. They dovetailed 1980s L.A. punk and 1920s Viennese coffeehouse culture, showcasing Vienna-Secession millwork, lighting pendants, and irregular geometric column tiles. Also featured are Judson Glass Studio's scaled up gothic stained glass and Simon and Nikki Haas's charcoal wall drawings representing celebrity culture, including Gloria Swanson standing on her head and the shaved head of Britney Spears.

NEW YORK (NY), UNITED STATES

GLASSERIE

DESIGN: SARA CONKLIN

I n GLASSERIE'S kitchen, the chef respects his ingredients and manipulates them as minimally as possible. So, too, does GLASSERIE'S interior. Located in the former Greenpoint Glass Works factory, built in 1860, the space feels as if it was restored, not designed. The team used wooden benches with original factory sub-flooring and exposed brick walls; light fixtures representative of those once made in the factory, whose illumination is measured in candle power; and prints that were taken from ancient glass fixture catalogues. GLASSERIE transports diners—who have already walked through a post-industrial neighborhood lost in time to get there—into an industrial Art Deco experience, complete with a wall of succulents.

DONNY'S BAR

DESIGN: LUCHETTI KRELLE

Sydney-based interior designers Stuart Krelle and Rachel Luchetti do many things, but hospitality is their forte. They made D O N N Y ' S B A R—situated in a benign coastal suburb called Manly—rustic, industrial, and urban while fusing Australian flavor with New York loft style and a Chinatown back alley. The challenge was to establish a balance of the cool and the friendly, the raw and the refined. Although the chef serves Asian-style tapas and dumplings, the two didn't rely on overtly Asian motifs; rather, they pared-down the interior, using a limited palette of materials including exposed brick, Edison bulbs, a spiral staircase, salvaged materials and furnishings, and extruded metal mesh. The result is an environment rich with texture but clear of clutter.

AN ENVIRONMENT
RICH WITH
TEXTURE
BUT CLEAR OF
CLUTTER

PIZZA WITH NO NAME

DESIGN: BAULHÚS

Under the name Baulhús, Hálfdan Lárus Pedersen does production design for motion pictures and interiors. In a similarly cinematic way, Pedersen designed PIZZA WITH NO NAME to feel strange, eclectic, dark, and cozy: "The house is, after all, very haunted," he points out. Starting with a former four-story residence, he transformed its multiple rooms into a pizzeria, including the basement and attic. Each room was given its own character with one shared feature: a lived-in atmosphere. This apparently produces no ordinary pizza: every ingredient is handmade from scratch at NO NAME, and the toppings are usually unusual.

HAWKSMOOR SPITALFIELDS BAR

DESIGN: MACAULAY SINCLAIR
AND HUW GOTT

Through a matte black brick doorway, HAWKSMOOR SPITALFIELDS is a cross between a gentleman's club and a grand old-school subway platform. The walls of a trio of alcoves are sheathed in luminous blue Art Nouveau tiles and hung with brass cage lights. The leather seats are navy and the walls peacock blue, while shiny copper tops the bar. In a basement that was once a strip club, the space has a subterranean feel and a sense of age due to the designers' choice of materials—tinted mirrors, teak parquet flooring, wooden tables that once served as chemistry lab counters, and a polished brass wall made from 90-year-old elevator doors. The doors were salvaged from the Unilever Building in Embankment, as were white Victorian glazed bricks used to clad the columns.

CAPE TOWN, SOUTH AFRICA

TRUTH COFFEE

DESIGN: HALDANE MARTIN

Martin's 1,500-square-meter TRUTH is a Steampunk-fueled future-retro Victorian fantasy. In a century-old warehouse, the café, barista trainee school, event space, coffee bean warehouse, espresso machine workshop, and offices are anchored by a 3-ton Probat roaster kitted out with circular steel shelving that recalls a Victorian gasworks. Martin exposed original cast iron pillars, Oregon pine roof trusses and floors, and preserved the patina of age, while adding raw steel, timber, leather, brass, and copper finishes. Over the communal table with swing-out stools, he floated flickering candle bulb lighting and a power cable installation that lets guests charge their gadgets. Even the restrooms and uniforms by Little Hattery, which Martin describes gleefully as "outlandish," are Steampunk.

129

A STEAMPUNK-FUELED
FUTURE-RETRO
VICTORIAN FANTASY

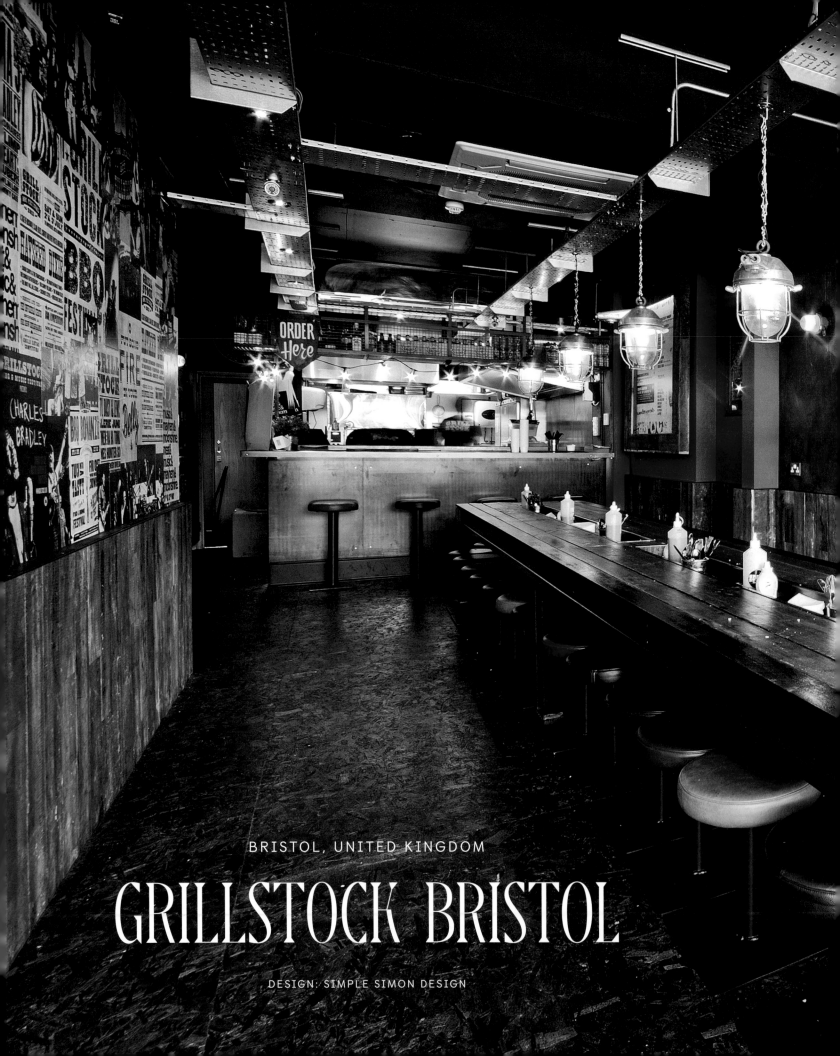

BRISTOL, UNITED KINGDOM

GRILLSTOCK BRISTOL

DESIGN: SIMPLE SIMON DESIGN

THE INTERIOR REFLECTS THE OWNERS' "MEAT, MUSIC AND MAYHEM" MANTRA.

GRILLSTOCK BRISTOL, a smokehouse modeled on a backyard barbecue, is owned by music festival producers who wanted the interior to reflect their "meat, music and mayhem" mantra. The 32-person communal table, built from steel girder, emphasizes the Deep Southern BBQ theme and echoes the festival's conviviality while conveniently maximizing seating capacity in a small space. Other bespoke furnishings, the counter, and gantry were made from blackened steel and exposed weld mesh. Tabletops and walls consist of rough sawn timber, and salvaged marine pendant lights live alongside neon signage. More rough elements deepen the space's character too: OSB board roughens the floor, rust crawls over the walls, and electrical service trays remain exposed on the ceiling.

BUNGENÄS KALKLADA→P.148 Bungenäs, Sweden

PROGRESSIVE

TEXT: SHONQUIS MORENO

The avant-garde interiors in the following pages involve experiments in concept, food, form, function, or all of the above. Often associated with one or multiple forms of art, they are pushing the envelope of food space and eating design in every direction.

The aptly named INFARM→P.140 is the apotheosis of indoor farming and its growing movement. INFARM represents a set of sustainable values rooted in a food movement and then translated into an interior that includes both a garden and a café. The café's kitchen looks as it might in any residential Berlin loft, but the living room has been taken over by a greenhouse. Its walls hold planters in floor-to-ceiling racks, and in a citified breakfast nook, irrigation tubes give hydroponic shelves the look of a benign laboratory experiment. This is an eating space that grows people and their values too. Likewise, the THREE BUNS→P.144 burger restaurant and bar is a light-filled volume that looks like a greenhouse for humans. After all, the owners have said that they want to provide relief from the urban condition. This outdoor-ish interior, planted with greenery, features simple communal seating made from tiered plywood platforms: people planters.

The L TRAIN DINNER PARTY→P.152 was part of the informal (read: unlicensed) nomadic supper club movement that has swept New York City and the globe for the last several years. It brought strangers with a passion for creative food practice together in the flesh. En route to Brooklyn from Manhattan on the L train which bores under the East River, the members of A Razor, A Shiny Knife, cooked, served, and essentially performed a refined but unconventional meal on custom-designed tables suspended from the ceiling. Beyond posing a black diamond challenge for the chef and servers, the dinner party also responded to a widespread craving for real human connection in real-time.

TADIOTO→P.146 looks like a jungle gym crossed with a tuk tuk. It is an experiment in assigning unconventional form to a contemporary food environment and in asking how passersby will use public space when no explicit function has been assigned to it. Geneva's Bureau A noticed that, in Hanoi, most objects live multiple lives because, out of necessity or resourcefulness, inhabitants recycle constantly and unconsciously. Bureau A based their bicycle-powered skeleton structure on the popular local bia hoi, or beer joint, but made it vertical, which is all the easier to pedal around. They also made it invitingly generic, so that while it may be used as drinking space, it might also become anything in the hands of inventive locals.

THE FOLLOWING PAGES INVOLVE EXPERIMENTS IN CONCEPT, FOOD, FORM, FUNCTION, OR ALL OF THE ABOVE

CONSTELLATIONS→P.138 is as much a work of art as it is an art, bar, garden, and eating space. Essentially a carpenterly sculpture by the Miller Brothers, its wooden canopy fronts the zagging brick gables of a historical warehouse with which it was designed to be in direct dialogue. Ten doubled A-frame structures support the swagging structure with an angular asymmetry while also doubling as benches and tables.

Not so much a formal as a structural experiment, the restaurant, bar, and art gallery BUNGENÄS KALKLADA→P.148 comprises a freestanding architecture that resembles a functional art installation. A series of plywood micro-art-itectures—glass doors, pine wood chairs, stools and tables, a cabinet-like washroom—are placed within the old shell of the architecture, in large part without touching it, and can be easily reconstructed, added onto, or removed with minimal impact.

EAST SIDE KING→P.154, on the other hand, is all about high impact. Conceived by Paul Qui and Moto Utsunomiya, it is a food truck and a confection of mobile art and artful combinations of flavors like the Sapporo beer bacon miso ramen. The truck looks as creative as the food tastes, a masterpiece of street art by Peelander Yellow, and embodies the creative freedom that the men apply to their unconventional ingredients. KARTEL→P.156 represents the creative freedom of street artists in Haifa. The entire building, an old boat hangar, was turned into a living canvas by Ghostown Crew to await the inspirations of other local and international artists and Djs. An all-in-one performance, art, eating, and meeting venue, it is run by the artists who rehabilitated the space—and who will transform it periodically at two-week intervals.

We love our virtual social spaces. In this chapter, however, the most experimental eating spaces make it clear that we will always crave a face-to-face, voice-to-voice, place-setting-to-place-setting reconnection—with other people and with our urge to move into the future, too.

CONSTELLATIONS BAR

DESIGN: H. MILLER BROS.

H ugh, a furniture designer and maker, and Howard, an architect, were asked to design the outdoor CONSTELLATIONS BAR, art space, and community garden situated in the ascendant creative quarter of Liverpool, the Baltic Triangle. Once a warehouse that burned down, the building's remaining gables helped them to establish the profile of the canopy, which was prefabricated in the brothers' workshop and assembled on-site in three days. Ten quadrapods—doubled A-Frame supports—made from green oak hold up the swagging structure and doubletask as benches or tables. The severe, asymmetrical angles of the canopy are a syncopated version of the worn brick roofline behind it, like a little architectural jazz.

INFARM

DESIGN: INFARM

oving on from those antiquated Soylent Green dystopias and past the bee-hives ranged across Brooklyn's roof-tops, Berlin's indoor farming movement is growing. I N F A R M is a vertical farming start-up offering urban communities a way to raise organic produce locally, season be damned. With Stockholm's Tomorrow Machine, they also offer a microgreen growing kit in a smartly designed origami-like packaging that can be folded into a miniature greenhouse of its own. Through transparent waterproof walls, observe microgreens in their own micro-architecture as they sprout.

LA CABUCHE

DESIGN: BUREAU A

Bureau A generate designs through abstract narratives imagined at the site. They compare LA CABUCHE, accessible by foot in the serene Swiss countryside, to David Lynch's notorious One-Eyed Jack, a fictional Canadian brothel. Like Lynch, Bureau A has a keen sense of the surreal qualities of ordinary life. In the radiant calm that palpably blankets the restaurant, visitors alternate between ease and malaise in the face of this rare repose. A diminutive ivy-clad stone house, it stands at the mouth of a vineyard, offering oenophiles a sanctuary from the city, within sight of the city. Extending from one flank of the existing classical building, a platform for terrace seating floats beneath an unnervingly cantilevered canopy, enhancing the sensation of troubling tranquility.

P OTATO HEAD'S →P.178 two owners want
to provide relief from the urban condition.
Collaborating with Thomas Hardian, Rovalino
Gultom, Ade Herkarisma, and Marius
Suntanu, they grew this semi-outdoor interior,
which (ware)houses a boutique burger restaurant
and cocktail bar. A vintage caravan marks the
spot where THREE BUNS yawns inward to a
generously light and space-filled area flanked with
greenery. Here, contemporary communal seating
consists of tiered plywood platforms where guests
sit, as if on bleachers, watching the dust motes in
peace. Community-building has rarely occurred
through cocktails, but THREE BUNS is not just a
house of spirits; it's an urban garden, a greenhouse
where human beings can photosynthesize too.

THREE BUNS

DESIGN: POTATO HEAD

145

HANOI, VIETNAM

TADIOTO

DESIGN: BUREAU A

According to Leopold Banchini and Daniel Zamarbide of Geneva-based Bureau A, "everything is dense in Hanoi, including the milk in your coffee." The Vietnamese city is also a place where most objects lead multiple lives because inhabitants practice constant, unconscious acts of up-cycling. This blue skeleton structure is Bureau A's version of the city's popular bia hoi, or beer joints, which spill into the streets. This vertical version of the beer joint was made for local art space TADIOTO and resembles a jungle gym crossed with a tuk tuk. The designers envisioned it as a convertible piece of mobile micro-architecture, bone without flesh which, perched atop three bicycle wheels, could become anything in the hands of resourceful Hanoi inhabitants.

BUNGENÄS KALKLADA

DESIGN: SKÄLSÖ ARKITEKTER

The hundred-year-old BUNGENÄS LIME BARN once provided storage at a limestone quarry. Abandoned in 1963, it lay quiescent in a landscape more derelict than its kilns, rearing up optimistically in a bald and thirsty spot, until its respectful, low-impact conversion into a restaurant, bar, and art gallery. A new layer of structures were grafted onto the barn, but are largely freestanding, easily reworked, and expandable at need. Floor-to-ceiling glass doors were tailored to the existing entry, harvesting light that fills the space. Pine wood chairs, stools, and tables were made by the architects, along with Kristoffer Sundin, to suit the large scale of the open interior; even the cabinet-like bathroom was crafted from plywood. The result is a new interior design that feels native to an old interior.

L-TRAIN DINNER PARTY

DESIGN: A RAZOR,
A SHINY KNIFE

The L train fishtails, threatening, or so it seems, to derail in the tunnel under the East River. It was on this route, and en route, from Manhattan to Brooklyn, that the culinary performers of A Razor, A Shiny Knife, served a 3-Michelin-star meal in a subway car. The goal was to choreograph—the public space, the acrobatic service, the delicacies served—a once-in-a-lifetime experience. Custom-designed tables were hung from the ceiling and held china, crystal, silver, flowers, and linens. The train-car setting contrasted with and perfectly suited the menu, which was about refinement punctuated with the unconventional: raw fish, hot soup poured tableside. The second course was foie en brioche. The fifth, a triple-crème cheese—frozen in liquid nitrogen and shattered into a soft snow.

EAST SIDE KING

DESIGN: EAST SIDE KING

Japanese hot dogs, beet home fries, and beef pho' boys (that's a pun) in a single bowl: Sapporo beer bacon miso ramen. All of these exuberantly original dishes can be found inside EAST SIDE KING'S "fast casual food truck," which, on the outside, is a masterpiece of street art by Peelander Yellow. East Side King was a project that was launched by Paul Qui and Moto Utsunomiya on a whim while both were working at the Houston restaurant Uchi and drawing on the influences of Asian cultures, rock bands, art, and Austin's laid-back, experimental, fun-loving vibe. The truck came to represent creative freedom to them and then, pretty fast and casually, it came to look like it too.

EXUBERANTLY ORIGINAL DISHES ON THE INSIDE, A MASTERPIECE OF STREET ART ON THE OUTSIDE

KARTEL

DESIGN: GHOSTOWN CREW

This multilevel street art, music, and design space has colonized a derelict boat hangar that was built during the 1970s. As the area was gradually returning to life, two crews of local street artists transfigured the architectural shell into a canvas that awaits the visions of local and international street artists, who have been making Haifa one of the go-to places for progressive nightlife and street art. Ghostown had been running a graffiti store, bar, kitchen, gallery space, and DJ nights at various locations. Establishing K A R T E L brought their collective creative pursuits together under a single roof. Versatile and handy, the crews did all the construction work themselves, and continue to modify the space every two weeks to give life to an evolving, breathing cultural space.

BERLIN, GERMANY

NEUE HEIMAT

DESIGN: NEUE HEIMAT

•HAPPY BELLY•
AUSTERN BAR

2 AUSTERN 5,-
MIT ZITRONE

1/2 DUTZEND AUSTERN
MIT ZITRONE 14,-

GEMISCHTE PLATTE
(FÜR 2 PERSONEN) MIT
FRANZÖSISCHEM
ROHMILCH KÄSE,
GÄNSERILETTE
& SCHINKEN SOWIE
BROT VON SIRONI 10,-

GRAPHIC SPACES

TEXT: SHONQUIS MORENO

Color and graphics are versatile tools in spatial design because they so viscerally link us to our senses and emotions. Hue and pattern can be used to conjure optical illusions of spaciousness or intimacy, or optical illusions that skew an interior to the point of (appearing to) alter its form, scale, and proportions. Color can manufacture dark moods and invoke bright wellness; graphical elements can clarify circulation or confound it. Both may evoke place, orienting one in space or transporting one out of space and time. They might generate texture, or become a source of distraction or a focal point. They can sharpen or muddy one's perceptions. They can even look "edible," making a restaurant feel as delicious as the food it serves, evoking the five tastes: sweet, sour, salty, bitter, and umami.

HUESO →P.190 is notable for its lack of color, or technically, its monolithic use of every color in one. The restaurant's facade is a white grid; inside, diners walk into a two-story chamber of curiosities that resembles an entirely white Abstract Expressionist collage. Cadena + Asociados Concept Design clad whitewashed, double-height, dining room walls floor-to-ceiling with an extraordinary collection of ordinary objects: kitchen implements and thousands of animal bones displayed in a hodge-podge of frames. The whiteness has a flattening, democratizing effect on the objects, and generates a haphazard texture throughout. The displays recall the rare curiosities of a seventeenth-century wunderkammer, the chamber of wonders where a vaster, more mysterious world was once categorized through the very personal lens of a collector in order to formulate new ways of viewing the cosmos. In HUESO, each object becomes the piece of a puzzle, making the restaurant a place of discovery visit after visit.

Located in Panama City, the AMERICAN TRADE HOTEL →P.174 by Commune features a South American brand of modernism, a sultry minimalism that is enriched by local materials, crafted objects, and most notably, a combination of color, texture, and pattern. Old-World floor tiles and wood paneling hint at a colonial past. Leather and rope-back chairs, and lush potted greenery establish a tropical motif that is carried over to cushions hung from the wall as backrests. These warmer elements establish the identity of a space that would otherwise have been a little too chilly to suit the climate outside.

In some of the projects in these pages, less is more and nature serves as a guide, but occasionally, more is more, and color and other visuals feel as man-made as a meatball. HUBBOX TRURO →P.166 took over the interior of an English church reinvented by Meor Design.

COLOR CAN MANUFACTURE DARK MOODS AND INVOKE BRIGHT WELLNESS; GRAPHICAL ELEMENTS CAN CLARIFY CIRCULATION OR CONFOUND IT

Inside, the complexion of the leather banquettes, salvaged wood floors, and cargo containers that form the rear wall recuses itself behind typographical collages and hand-painted murals that mimic the appearance of signage, bright and welcomingly naive in their aesthetic. The tiling of saturated colors in a mural dominating the main dining room recalls stained glass, playing on the rosette window still visible from the street, and exuberantly nodding to the space's former incarnation as a house of God.

If less is more and more is more depending on the context, more isn't even remotely enough in MEAT LIQUOR BRIGHTON →P.196, an English nightclub where Shed collaged and tattooed the black surfaces of walls, floors, and ceilings with a riot of backlit graphics. To do this, the designers brought insistent, overwhelming color and imagery in from the surrounding Brighton fairgrounds so that in this interior, they evoke place—surreal, vociferous, layered, and immersive.

BIBO →P.164 lies somewhere between these extremes. This faceted glass Hong Kong boîte is also a contemporary gallery, which makes it all the colors of the art that rotates through it. In a studied way, by the time the designers at Substance were finished designing the interior, the restaurant felt unfinished—in order to be completed, and not overwhelmed by the wide range of artworks passing through. Ephemeral and serendipitous then, the complexion of the space is carried in and taken out with the canvases on show; it dribbles down the wall from a spray paint can in crude graffiti tags or laces a column with primary colors.

IZAKAYA KINOYA →P.180 by Jean de Lessard embraces a material rawness that is well-suited to the character of the typical sake and beer bar; it is nailed together crudely from timber planks of various tones and finishes and graffitied in Japanese. But this izakaya is not just casual and carpenterly, fit for a bayou or a barn. The diverse finishes of the planks stripe the room with an exaggerated graphic quality, while its splintery coarseness is sculptural in the extreme. The interior walls are so deeply faceted that they form intimate niches.

At KINOYA, the graphical quality is, in large part, a method for organizing and animating space, but it is also a gustatory expression of the spirits and brews: earthy, shape-shifting, deep, and full of texture. In all these spaces, color and graphics amplify the taste of our food and drink and heighten the sharpness or mellowness of the way we experience conviviality. They let us taste our senses and emotions. They let us taste where we are. As flavors are to the tongue, color and graphics are to the eye—and emotion is the product of both of them.

BIBO

DESIGN: SUBSTANCE

Substance calls themselves "a collective of people with imaginations so far-reaching that if we were a single hybrid person you would probably be afraid to be our friend." BIBO is a Boho-inflected take on an urban French Art Deco fine-dining boîte, and a canvas for contemporary and street art. The 1930s aesthetic is modern enough to frame a constantly changing and always eclectic presentation of art, while making for an elegant eatery. To make raw artwork feel at home, they gave BIBO an organically unfinished look. The gem-shaped glazed box of the facade creates intriguing views in or out. "Our productivity is not purely achieved by sitting at the desk," the designers will tell you. "Napping for the explicit reason of conjuring surreal ideas is completely justifiable." BIBO is the proof.

TO MAKE
RAW ARTWORK
FEEL AT HOME,
THEY GAVE BIBO AN
ORGANICALLY
UNFINISHED LOOK

TRURO, UNITED KINGDOM

HUBBOX TRURO

DESIGN: MEOR STUDIO

Unusual word, HUBBOX. Look it up in a dictionary, and it will not say "a collision of the industrial and ecclesiastical"—but it should. Meor turned its 2D branding and web design skills into a hypergraphical 3D restaurant interior with the help of mural artist David Shillinglaw. An industrial, "American dirty diner" with an upcycled look and feel, the eatery had outgrown its original location in a shipping container, and is now located in a nineteenth-century Wesleyan church. Meor mixed up American 1950s diner iconography, 1980s New York Pop and graffiti art, the color schemes of Russian abstract painter Wassily Kandinsky, and Eastern European factory fittings and lighting to go with the original buttresses and stained glass.

AN INDUSTRIAL,
"AMERICAN DIRTY
DINER" WITH AN
UPCYCLED LOOK AND
FEEL

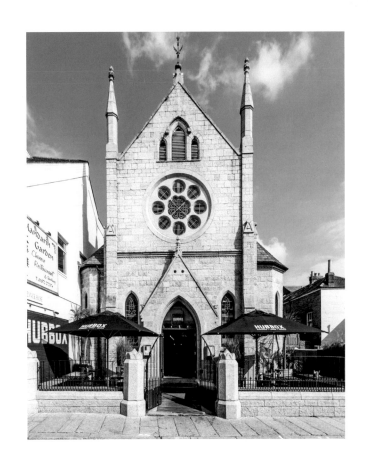

CLUB RESTAURANT BANANAS

DESIGN: YOLANDA VILALTA & HELENA JAUMÁ

This international Caribbean eatery is about "locura divertida" or "funny craziness," which reflects the eclecticism of its menu. Looking onto the 100-year-old market Mercat del Born, the interior is a patchwork of red, white, and blue tabletops, concrete floor tiles, woven plastic chairs, and a back of bar the color of a clown's nose. Another wall is also glowing—with neon palm trees—while, against the patio wall, hanging wicker egg chairs swing to and fro. Vilalta and Jaumá designed with humor, bringing in parrots (wall drawings) and leopards (or at least leopard upholstery). They also divided the space so that colored lighting can be altered and tables reconfigured to carve a dance floor out of what feels like a jungle circus. And then they made it as soundproof as it is bananas.

VILALTA AND JAUMÁ DESIGNED WITH HUMOR,

BRINGING IN PARROTS (WALL DRAWINGS)

AND LEOPARDS (OR AT LEAST LEOPARD UPHOLSTERY)

PANAMA CITY, PANAMA

AMERICAN TRADE HOTEL

DESIGN: COMMUNE DESIGN

The AMERICAN TRADE HOTEL comprises a patchwork of histories that nonetheless looks seamless. A 1920s building in the historic Casco Viejo neighborhood, it is a cocktail of architectural styles newly defined by a fictional narrative about a family-run luxury hotel once thrumming with correspondents, tycoons, artists, and musicians, each of whom have left a trace of themselves within. The new interiors are a mish-mash of twentieth-century styles: Austrian secessionist, Mexican modernist, Italian postmodern. Spanish Colonial, Hacienda style, the speakeasy, and back-alley New Orleans nightclubs are featured along with 1960s Mexican and Danish modern furniture. In the lobby café, a 1950s ice cream parlor collides with a tropical Havana nightclub and Harry Bertoia furniture.

THE JOHN DORY

DESIGN: ROMAN AND WILLIAMS

Pop, playful, quirky—this oyster bar's interior underscores the novelty of its chef's menu. Perhaps the brightest and lightest space designed by Roman and Williams, it feels almost tropical in its joy. The restaurant has its head in the Caribbean and its feet on the Manhattan pavement, grounded by a beautifully preserved original mosaic floor. THE JOHN DORY stands in stark contrast to the low-lit, wood-surfaced BRESLIN →P.112 that the couple designed for the Ace Hotel steps away. The space shines as light flowing in from the windows illuminates the copper table tops and sconces made from seashells. Even the black tile walls are lustrous. Effulgent emerald green and electric blue stools line the high bar, which is flanked by two oversize fish tanks—precisely where the flat-screen TVs would have hung in a sports bar.

POTATO HEAD FOLK

DESIGN: POTATO HEAD

POTATO HEAD spaces, as suggested by the name, are nothing if not whimsical, but they're sophisticatedly whimsical—urbane escapes from the urban. POTATO HEAD FOLK offers four distinct destinations in one—a pair of restaurants, a pair of bars—designed to have one thing in common: to feel like home. In this sanctuary for the local creative class (partly inspired by 1930s children's book illustrations), the first floor is an analog to the kitchen: a burger warehouse called THREE BUNS. On the second floor, the living room becomes a restaurant with table service. On the third floor is a drinking den, replete with wingback chairs, while on the roof, a garden opens up into an open-air bar strung with fairy lights.

179

IZAKAYA KINOYA

DESIGN: JEAN DE LESSARD

A udacious and rustic pretty much sum up the faceted, super-3D wooden interior of IZAKAYA KINOYA. Originally a casual sake and beer boite, it is transformed in the hands of de Lessard and Alexa Adam. Inside the existing black box of the first restaurant, the designers set a second, interior box. The splintered-looking surfaces of the inner box, with their chalky stripes and unfinished finishes, underscore the new eatery's formally extreme design. The outer box was envisioned as a threshold between the familiar city outside and the unanticipated architecture-inside-the-architecture. The deep fractal geometry of the inside walls establishes nooks that border on confining, but instead allow diners to feel tucked

SHUSTOV

DESIGN: DENIS BELENKO DESIGN BAND

D enis Belenko Design Band sounds a little Robin Hood, but is actually a collective of architects, artists, and designers who custom design and manufacture their own interior elements. From furniture and lighting to hydraulic tiles and églomisé or gilded glass, they combine with machine-making. The Band created this brandy bar in Odessa through a clever use of repetition and the combination of similar brown tones in varying materials. The monolithically amber tunnel space features circular barrel lids unevenly overlain from floor to rounded ceiling to floor again. Herringbone red brick floors look as if the designers had poured in the brandy itself. Patrons feel immersed, which is pretty much how drinking at a good bar works.

SABOTEN RESTAURANT

DESIGN: 4N ARCHITECTS

4N's design of this rope-riddled restaurant draws a profound distinction between texture and space. The shell of the interior is either red lacquer, which limns the space with color, or timber, which provides continuity between the ceiling panels and the finishes outside the room. Lengths of maritime rope serve as curtains and partitions that hang from ceiling to floor. The two designers organized seating meticulously to take advantage of the views outside. The effect of this dovetailing of traditional Japanese architecture with unconventional materials makes the space both cozy and mysterious.

SCHUITEMAKER VIS

DESIGN: DIRK VAN BERKEL

At 85 years old, this seafood restaurant has been run by family for generations, going back to the days of catching the fish themselves. Van Berkel showcases craftsmanship in his interiors, and all the materials he used here are associated with fishing and fish processing. Ship's rope stretches across the building, fastened to fine hooks, and is used as curtains. Shop lighting is bright and precise to make the staff's work easier and showcase the fish. In the restaurant, soft lighting and a warm look prevail. Van Berkel partitioned the two with racks of oak herring barrels that are also used as retail display for wine bottles and oils. The fish display case recalls a modern museum vitrine—which seems fitting for a living legacy.

LOS ANGELES (CA), UNITED STATES

UPSTAIRS AT THE ACE DTLA

DESIGN: COMMUNE DESIGN

This downtown bar is part of the eclectic, glossy and exuberantly tiled L.A. CHAPTER →P.114 restaurant below it, also by Commune. An open box guarded by a pair of mammoth concrete columns, it sits beneath a ceiling strung with bare bulbs and swagging lengths of metal chain of all weights, thicknesses, and degrees of oxidation. In the open space, a seating area is defined by art: a wall hanging made from felt blankets by Tanya Aguiñiga, and a cedar stump table and two taut leather Mexican butacas (armchairs) by sculptor Alma Allen. Lighting fixtures and awnings were also made by artists and mixed with whitewashed Mexican Equipale seating. The beat-up concrete in which the smooth wooden box of the bar floats looks spare at first glance, but turns out to be a showcase for local creatives and authentic materials.

189

HUESO

DESIGN: CADENA + ASOCIADOS CONCEPT DESIGN

Concept restaurant H U E S O enjoys a central location between the Luis Barragan Foundation and Diaz Morales's House-Studio in the Lafayette Design District. Alfonso Cadena renovated a 1940s building here, creating a layered shell. Outside, a graphical grid of artisanal white ceramic tiles clads the facade; inside, white objects are framed and ranged across monolithically whitewashed brick perimeter walls. Fired with a Darwinian fascination for collection and categorization, Cadena created this cabinet of curiosities, rife with texture. More than 10,000 animal bones, skulls, and sketches of skulls are mounted along with cutlery and kitchen implements up to the high ceilings. Butcher block communal tables and bentwood chairs look almost fleshy against the white surfaces.

Add big murals, some Japanese calligraphy, and brick-oven pizza to a warehouse atelier and you have ARTISAN, which fills a 1,115-square-meter quasi-industrial loft space in the Spinningfields district. To complement an interior by Michelle Derbyshire—a moodily low-lit space with exposed, old wooden coffers and beams, slatted lampshades, particleboard floors, and bent metal rod dining chairs that look like drawings of themselves—artist and illustrator Stephen Smith hand-painted black-and-white murals at the entrance foyer, stairway, and on the pizza-oven walls. Smith used typographic elements on the walls and Japanese-inflected brushstrokes on dining-room partitions. He then collaborated with local office Europa to create a corresponding identity, including the chicly graphic menus.

ARTISAN KITCHEN AND BAR

DESIGN: MICHELLE DERBYSHIRE

195

MEAT LIQUOR BRIGHTON

DESIGN: SHED.

I f The Illustrated Man was a bar: Shed tattooed the walls and ceiling of this 300-square-meter seascape eatery in images suggesting Brighton's unique charm. The colorful, overlain interior themes abut each other over a black background in a crush of references to the dynamism and electric-eclectic sensibility of Brighton's surreal fairgrounds, which Shed describes as "garish and sometimes sinister." The psychedelic result resembles a 1970s black-light poster in 3D: "We wanted to ensure we brought every inch of Brighton's energy into these interiors," the designers explain. That they did, immersively.

DRAMATIC

TEXT: SHONQUIS MORENO

In the following chapter, glamorous interiors have become less remote and less predictable. They are still decidedly lush and sophisticated, but they may also showcase less precious elements, handcrafted or industrial or idiosyncratic, that become precious in combination. They become an alloy—steel and silk, the past and the present, fiber optics and the flash of a cut diamond—a sleek armature of glam.

At OLD TOM & ENGLISH→P.248, glamor is not merely retro; it's a temporal hybrid that feels entirely up-to-date. Lee Broom mixes contemporary speakeasy with the living room and the English gentleman's club, set in spaces that feel discreet without being isolated, that offer escape with companionship. Nothing casts such a glamorous aura as having a secret to keep—it's just that no one wants to keep it alone. Here, Broom paints the town red. Using lipstick-red carpet, he underlines rooms that are otherwise burnished with low lighting and nobly neutral, subdued in pewter gray upholstery, grainy mid-tone woods, brass, and marble. With simple gestures, he dispenses with ornament but not serifs, opting for strong geometric forms—circular mirrors and hearths, globe lamps, and cylindrical fixtures placed diagonally. Striking a balance between masculine and feminine, he invokes the most powerful, contemporary qualities of each.

While technology may feel magical, designers have long worked more low-tech magic by exploiting grandeur of scale and form. These make the experience of a space feel larger-than-life, a feeling amplified today by the removal, not the addition, of flourishes. In THE PRESS CLUB→P.202, March Studio exaggerates scale, repeats basic forms, and limits the range of finishes to bridge minimal and rational with organic and luxe. Its color and materials palettes are sophisticated and neutral, limited to camel-colored leather upholstery, blond wood, and a perforated brass ceiling: modular, monolithically applied, and dramatically sculptural. In Sidharta's CARPE DIEM→P.222, opulent scale makes even rattan glamorous. Molded into a voluptuous column, a bench on the first floor rises through the ceiling and morphs into a bar on the floor above.

PPAG Architects gave the STEIRERECK IM STADTPARK→P.226 restaurant a thoroughly modern novelty. The reflective facades of several spare, boxy pavilions are clustered like gems amidst a park,

juxtaposing the playground outside with a grown-up interior. Their vertically sliding glazed walls have an avant-garde look and function, while an abstract tiling scheme provides an otherwise serene interior with staccato accents.

GLAMOROUS INTERIORS ARE STILL DECIDEDLY LUSH AND SOPHISTICATED, BUT THEY MAY ALSO SHOWCASE LESS PRECIOUS ELEMENTS THAT BECOME PRECIOUS IN COMBINATION.

Moving from bright to dark in Hong Kong, Joyce Wang has mastered moody glamor in her narrative interiors. AMMO→P.214 tells the story of the site's history as a munitions depot through a battery of steely textures. Stylt Trampoli tells stories based on context and through carefully curated objects as well. In a plush, detailed scenography, the aristocratic glamor

of GOTTHARDS KROG→P.210 is based on a mashup of eclectic objects—a skull, sea shells under a glass dome, a ship's lantern—that evokes the life of a gentleman turned sailor, depicting his historical personality as much as a contemporary space.

Studio Piet Boon also juxtaposes old and new in THE JANE's→P.230 emotive interior. In a monumental former church, its ceilings reach so high as to inspire thoughts of the architects as much as the heavens. Surfaces used with devotion through generations contrast succinctly with modern furnishings, especially a vast radiating chandelier—scaled to the volume of the dining room—whose multitude of spindly black arms end in glass globes, recalling a Copernican model of the solar system. It bespeaks the creativity of a culture rising from the depths and into the light, celebrating the wonders of a world that both God and man had wrought. That is, of course, what glamor is: the mysterious mundane touched by the charismatic and the sublime.

THE PRESS CLUB

DESIGN: MARCH STUDIO

In fine dining, food is laboriously hand-crafted. Its artisans consider the composition of each dish at the most granular—even molecular—level and as it pertains to each of the senses. In much the same way, March approached THE PRESS CLUB interior, a study in neutral hues from camel to brass. Collared in semicircular booths, the tables were rendered in blond wood, supple leather, and nude tones. The ceiling, organized as a textural brass hierarchy, cascades from a mirrored wall to the glazed facade, resembling an upside-down forest of hand-folded brass cylinders and trumpets. It also serves to hide mechanical services, spotlights, and grille-covered speakers. The effect is deliciously textured, supremely coherent, and richly material, making the ceiling as important as the dining room below it.

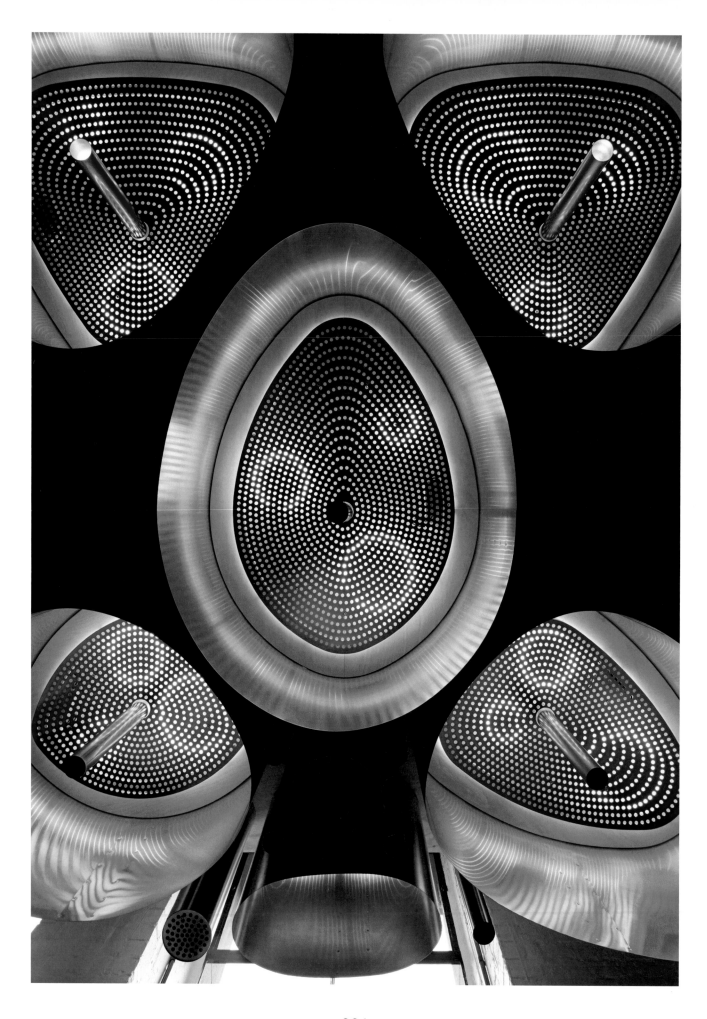

MOTT 32

DESIGN: JOYCE WANG

This cinematic interior walks guests, literally, through the story of an immigrant changing stations in life. The tale is told in dark rooms—one big and five discrete, and discreet, smaller ones—rich with glossy black lacquer, family heirlooms, and moody details. The private rooms have distinct identities assigned by objects and finishes, including Mahjong-style dining tables, a bar resembling an apothecary cabinet, and an abacus-inspired chandelier. Graffiti filigrees the columns, Chinese paint-brushes wallpaper the Tangerine Room, and surfaces are deeply textured, using screens, embossed glass, and offset brick. Crowning the dining room, a dramatic architectural "skylight" bathes guests in daylight, whatever the hour. The denouement? A room with door handles shaped like those of a bank vault.

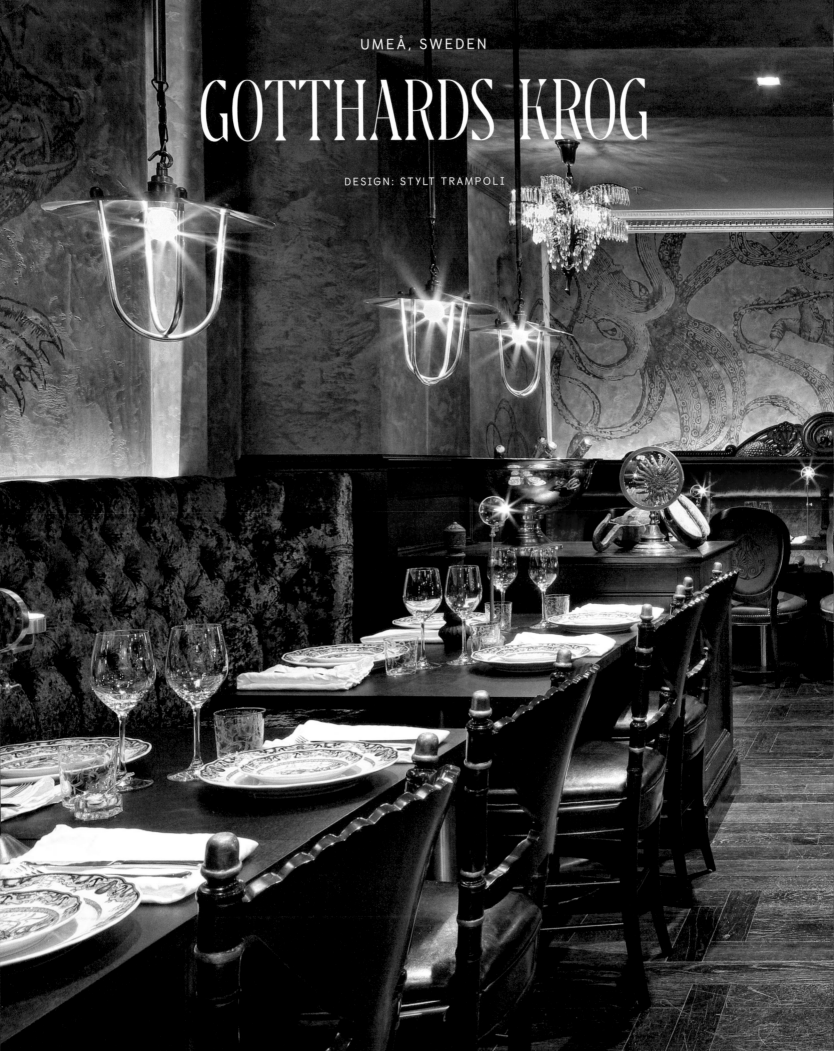

UMEÅ, SWEDEN

GOTTHARDS KROG

DESIGN: STYLT TRAMPOLI

At heart, Erik Nissen Johansen is a theater scenographer with a gothically rococo and detailed imagination, inside which anyone should want to eat dinner. GOTTHARDS KROG, in a "saltwater-scented grand hotel," is named after the much-storied first proprietor, Gotthard Zetterberg, about whom it is difficult to distinguish fact from fiction. And so it is with this interior. In 1883, Gotthard sailed with a renowned explorer to find out if any part of Greenland was, in fact, green—a failed venture that nonetheless turned Gotthard into a sailor at heart. The interior is plush and rough, celebratory and morbid: a carved skull crowns the velvet sofa, octopuses ink up the wallpaper, and ships' lanterns dimly illuminate seashell trophies and a trumpet wedged into the bartop.

AMMO

DESIGN: JOYCE WANG

Another of storyteller Joyce Wang's cinematic interiors, AMMO draws on the historical, architectural, and cultural significance of its site, a nineteenth-century explosives magazine compound, which was converted into the Asia Society Hong Kong Center by Tod Williams and Billie Tsien. Looking to the film noir Alphaville, the restaurant features three sculptural spiral staircases made from copper plumbing pipes that serve as chandeliers. The ceiling recalls a bunker and Wang favored materials associated with both industry and the military. She often designs furniture and fixtures exclusively for a project, in silk, leather, and velvet. Together, velvet and leather convey a lush luxury and provide counterpoint to the harder, chillier elements of the design.

PAK LOH CHIU CHOW

DESIGN: NC DESIGN & ARCHITECTURE

Trained in both architecture and fashion, Nelson Chow has taken the industrial upbringing he had while working for AvroKO in New York City and refined it with the residential and yacht design he did for Edge Design Institute. In spite of its long history and its famed, traditional Chiu Chow cuisine, PAK LOH caters to evolving modern tastes by adding atypical ingredients to long-familiar dishes. Taking their cue, NCDA blended tradition with innovation by stirring together allusions to bygone and modern materials. Chow privileged abstraction over Chinese vernacular with a remarkable vaulted, finned ceiling structure and arcing, fluted walls, while still creating a synthesis of classic and contemporary elements.

CARPE DIEM BAR AND RESTAURANT

DESIGN: SIDHARTA ARCHITECT

This sculptural restaurant offers some formal poetry—organic forms mix with clean lines, and tight curves become highly graphical. But the space was designed for a rather prosaic purpose: to showcase the equally sculptural and masterfully crafted Yamakawa brand rattan furniture in a living setting. At the center of a void on the second floor, Sidharta displays the bar like an artwork. Sheathed in rattan, it cascades to the floor below, where it crests into a bench for guests waiting to be seated. The environment is slathered with super-textural natural materials, patterned 3D wooden or plank walls, and wicker juxtaposed with poured concrete walls, which were molded in wood-plank frames. The spiral staircase, flanked with dark rattan, illustrates not just the skill, but the ranging modernity of Yamakawa's artisans.

223

STEIRERECK IM STADTPARK

DESIGN: PPAG ARCHITECTS

S TEIRERECK'S design starts with the dining table and works its way outward. Innovations include the placement of tables in niches and huge, single-pane electric sash windows that slide up and down. They open onto courtyards beside the pavilions, which have burnished, almost mirrored, steel facades. These and the finger-like organization of the pavilions give a sense of proximity to the adjacent park and playground. The facade material drips like mercury into the interior, creating metal panels that can be rotated to create rooms of various dimensions. The tiers of a floating drop ceiling that resembles a topographical map allow it to navigate the varying heights of the panels. STEIRERECK'S design makes a strong statement—but in hushed, melodic tones.

228

ANTWERP, BELGIUM

THE JANE

DESIGN: STUDIO PIET BOON

Fine dining meets rock n' roll in THE JANE, which was commissioned by 3-star Michelin chef Sergio Herman, along with chef Nick Bril. Oostzaan-based Studio Piet Boon transmuted the chapel attached to a former military hospital in Antwerp into a high-end contemporary eatery. Boon's design team sought authenticity, high-functionality, and materials that improve with age. The studio chose to restore only what was necessary in the chapel—the ceiling for instance—and then deck out the rest in contemporary elements. Perhaps in a symbolic gesture, the glass-wrapped kitchen replaces the altar, creating a shrine in which food preparation becomes transparent to the guests.

LJUBLJANA, SLOVENIA

LOLITA

DESIGN: TRIJE ARHITEKTI

Located in a former depot on the grounds of a palace, LOLITA pays homage to the café tradition, which in its turn, celebrates the joie de vivre that created the café in the first place. Like big, wondering eyes, LOLITA'S windows fill the café with light. The parquet floor represents a dovetailing of century-old tiles and new colored elements. Five meters overhead, dominating the room, the ceiling is a collage, depicting the allegory of Venus and Apollo overlain with an image of a traditional woman's handkerchief and a detail from Gustav Doré's painting The Creation of Eve. A flat chandelier, shaped like a burning cross, hangs from the ceiling in front of a brick wall and casts a white shadow while doilie-like and cherry-shaped lamps by Nika Zupanc punctuate the sweetly precocious interior.

SUPERSENSE

DESIGN: SUPERSENSE

S UPERSENSE was designed by Florian Kaps and his collaborators to spoil all the senses with an old-fashioned splendor free from extraneous frills. A concept shop, café, bar, workshop and more, SUPERSENSE is the brainchild of a small team directed by the founder of The Impossible Project, who is also known for rescuing the last Polaroid factory. The interiors recall the grandeur of a palace for good reason: they occupy a building designed and built in 1898 by Carl Caufal, whose architecture was inspired by the spirit of Venice.

CHRISTOPHER'S

DESIGN: DE MATOS RYAN

L ondon's De Matos Ryan went all out to make CHRISTOPHER'S interior opulent, sumptuous, ornate, and luxurious—unabashedly bucking the trend, in uncertain economic times, toward austerity. The restaurant harks back to the halcyon days of glamor embodied in the existing building by drawing on materials and finishes with the classiest pedigree, like marble and brass. CHRISTOPHER'S offers three discrete areas for drinking and dining: a ground-floor Martini Bar featuring cocktails and informal dining, a dining room; on the first floor; and a club room for private events on the lower ground. Even if only slightly different, each space has a distinct spirit. Coherence and continuity are maintained through the establishment of a consistent materials palette.

TOM DIXON SANDWICH, HARRODS

DESIGN: DESIGN RESEARCH STUDIO & TOM DIXON

Tom Dixon furnished SANDWICH with pieces from his eponymous range, showcasing his prolific output of brass lighting fixtures, upholstered club chairs, and marble-covered tables. The designers ranged black tiles in brickwork patterns along the face of the counter, anchored with fixed purple seating and color-matched moveable chairs. To partition the space into three zones, they used seating of different styles and colors as well as various lighting schemes. A casual area welcomes visitors with generous wing-backed armchairs and smaller lounge seats. Lustre pendant lights hang from the ceiling in sets of four.

TO PARTITION
THE SPACE
INTO THREE ZONES,
THEY USED SEATING
OF DIFFERENT
STYLES AND COLORS
AS WELL AS
VARIOUS LIGHTING
SCHEMES

ECLECTIC

DESIGN: DESIGN RESEARCH STUDIO

T he name says it all: just as the menu unites disparate influences, so too the interior. The design team mixed the restaurant with its modernist surroundings and Parisian chic with British eccentricity, creating an homage to 1970s architecture and a more private brasserie experience. Concrete was used in multiple textures: unfinished, waxed, alternately bare and blanketed with thick carpet to create moments of warmth. Hexagons, visible in many details, recall the 1970s. Lighting always equals mood in Creative Director Tom Dixon's work: here, various lamps control lighting precisely, intensifying the hues of textiles and upholstery. Sculptural furnishings organize the room, and the mash-up of highbrow details and finishes renders the space less imposing but still grand.

OLD TOM & ENGLISH

DESIGN: LEE BROOM

This tiny basement bar and restaurant features intimate dining nooks, low light, and plush furnishings. The theatrical aspects of entertaining at home during the 1960s are paired with contemporary riffs. Corresponding with the emphasis on traditional English dishes and high-class bar culture—Old Tom is an eighteenth-century lowball—guests enter through a slatted wooden door and hidden hatch to the bar, lounge, or one of five "personal cloisters" named after celebrated ladies of the night. Broom used shades of gray, flashes of scarlet carpet, brass, oak, his cut-glass Crystal Bulb and his marble lighting collection. The ultimate luxury? Each zone boasts its own old-school bar service—a sideboard, revolving cocktail cabinet, or bar cart—from which waiters furnish the cocktails.

INDEX

DESIGNER A–Z

March Studio
Australia
www.marchstudio.com.au
← P. 202 THE PRESS CLUB
www.thepressclub.com.au
Photos: Peter Bennetts

Marshall Projects
United States
www.marshall-projects.com
← P. 110 GJELINA
www.gjelina.com
Designer: Sam Marshall
Photos: Robb Aaron Gordon

Masquespacio
Spain
www.masquespacio.com
← P. 66 VINO VERITAS
ECO-GASTROBAR
www.vinoveritasoslo.com
Photos: David Rodríguez
& Carlos Huecas

Mathieu Lehanneur
France
www.mathieulehanneur.fr
← P. 24 CAFÉ ARTSCIENCE
www.cafeartscience.com
Photos: Phase One Photography

Meor Studio
United Kingdom
www.meorstudio.co.uk
← P. 166 HUBBOX TRURO
www.hubbox.co.uk
Additional credits: David Shillinglaw
(Mural artist)
Photos: Matthew Heritage

Michelle Derbyshire
United Kingdom
www.michellederbyshire.com
← P. 194 ARTISAN KITCHEN
AND BAR
www.artisan.uk.com
Additional credits: Neasden Control
Centre (Artwork)
www.neasdencontrolcentre.com
Photos: James Brown Photography

MM18 Arquitetura
Brazil
www.mm18.com.br
← P. 82 RAMONA
www.casaramona.com.br
Photos: Pedro Vanucchi

NC Design & Architecture Ltd.
China
www.ncda.biz
← P. 220 PAK LOH CHIU
CHOW
Additional credits: Whatever Workshop
(Graphic Design)
Photos: Nathaniel McMahon

Neue Heimat
Germany
www.neueheimat.com
← P. 158 NEUE HEIMAT
Photos: Zoë Noble, Thang Dia and
Sasha Kharchenko

Note
Sweden
www.notedesignstudio.se
← P. 58 FINEFOOD KÄRLEK
OCH MAT
www.finefood.se
Photos: Note

NOTHING SOMETHING
United States
www.nothingsomething.com
← P. 108 SMOKESTACK
AT MAGNOLIA BREWERY
www.magnoliasmokestack.com
Designer: Kevin Landwehr
Additional credits: Devin Becker
(Production Design)
Photos: Eric Wolfinger (P. 108),
Leslie Santarina/Spotted SF (P. 109)

Onion Co.,Ltd.
Thailand
www.onion.co.th
← P. 30 SALA RATTANAKOSIN
EATERY AND BAR
www.salaresorts.com/rattanakosin
Designer: Siriyot Chaiamnuay
& Arisara Chaktranon
Additional credits: M. L. Chittawadi
Chitrabongs (Text)
Photos: Wison Tungthunya,
W Workspace

PB/Studio
Poland
www.p-bstudio.com
← P. 84 ALTHAUS
RESTAURANT
www.restauracjaalthaus.pl
Designer: PB/Studio & Filip Kozarski
Photos: TOMiRRi Photography

Potato Head
Indonesia
www.ptthead.com
← P. 144 THREE BUNS
www.threebuns.com
Designer: Ronald Akili, Jason Gunawan,
Thomas Hardian, Rovalino Gultom, Ade
Herkarisma, and Marius Suntanu
Photos: Davy Linggar
← P. 178 POTATO HEAD FOLK
www.pttheadfolk.com
Designer: Ronald Akili, Jason Gunawan,
and Takenouchi Webb
Additional designer: David Bromley
Photos: Amos Wong

PPAG architects ztgmbh
Austria
www.ppag.at
← P. 228 STEIRERECK IM
STADTPARK
www.steirereck.com
Photos: Helmut Pierer

Roman and Williams
United States
www.romanandwilliams.com
← P. 112 THE BRESLIN
www.thebreslin.com
Photos: Nicole Franzen
← P. 176 THE JOHN DORY
OYSTER BAR
www.thejohndory.com
Additional designer: Ken Friedman
Additional credits: Melissa Hom,
Daniel Krieger
Photos: Nicole Franzen

Rum4
Denmark
www.rum4.dk
← P. 56 MIKKELLER
& FRIENDS
www.mikkeller.dk
Designer: Karsten K. & Kristian Lillelund/
Rum4
Photos: Camilla Stephan
& Rasmus Malmstrøm

Sara Conklin
United States
← P. 116 GLASSERIE
www.glasserienyc.com
Additional designer: C. Wall Architecture,
Space Exploration
Photos: Remy Amezcua

Shed.
United Kingdom
www.shed-design.com
← P. 196 MEAT LIQUOR
BRIGHTON
www.meatliquor.com
Photos: James Medcraft

Sidharta Architect
Indonesia
www.sidhartaarchitect.com
← P. 224 CARPE DIEM BAR
AND RESTAURANT
www.carpediem-yamakawa.com
Photos: Fernando Gomulya

Simple Simon Design
United Kingdom
www.simplesimondesign.co.uk
← P. 132 GRILLSTOCK
BRISTOL
www.grillstock.co.uk
Photos: Frances Taylor

Skälsö Arkitekter
Sweden
www.skalso.se
← P. 148 BUNGENÄS
KALKLADA
www.bungenas.se
Photos: Anna Sundström

Studio Piet Boon
Netherlands
www.pietboon.com
← P. 232 THE JANE
www.thejaneantwerp.com
Photos: Richard Powers

Stylt Trampoli AB
Sweden
www.stylt.se
←—P. 214 GOTTHARDS KROG
www.gotthardskrog.se
Photos: Erik Nissen Johansen

Substance
Hong Kong
www.aworkofsubstance.com
←—P. 164 BIBO
www.bibo.hk
Photos: Red Dog (P. 164 bottom),
Nathaniel McMahon (P. 164 top, P. 165)

SUPERSENSE
Austria
←—P. 240 SUPERSENSE
the.supersense.com
Designer: Florian Kaps/Supersense
Additional designer: Andreas Eduard
Hoeller, Nina Ugrinovich
Additional credits: Marco Christian Krenn
Photos: Gebhard Sengmüller

Taller KEN
Guatemala
www.tallerken.info
←—P. 88 SAUL ZONA 14
www.saulemendez.com
Designer: Ines Guzman,
Gregory Melitonov
Photos: Andreas Asturias

**Terry Sawyer and
John Finger**
United States
←—P. 106 HOG ISLAND
OYSTER FARM
www.hogislandoysters.com
Additional designer: Erik Schlagenhauf,
Garret Hamner
Photos: Leslie Santarina/Spotted SF

THEZIMMER
Germany
www.thezimmer.de
←—P. 100 FLEISCHEREI
Designer: Michael Grzesiak
Additional designer: Sebastian Stiess
Photos: photographiedepot

+tongtong
Canada
www.tongtong.co
←—P. 42 HER MAJESTY'S
PLEASURE
www.hermajestyspleasure.ca
Additional designer: John Tong and
Kateryna Nebesna
Additional credits: Steven Fong
Architect (Architect of Record); Gaydon
Contractors Ltd. (Contractor)
Photos: Lisa Petrole

Trije arhitekti
Slovenia
www.trijearhitekti.si
←—P. 238 LOLITA
www.slascicarna-lolita.si
Designer: Andrej Mercina/Trije arhitekti
Additional designer: Jagoda Jejčič
Photos: Miran Kambič

Wibke Isenberg-Cohen
Germany
←—P. 96 SALUMERIA LAMURI
www.salumerialamuri.de
Additional designer: Ania Osko
(Assistant)
Photos: Federico Testa

Workstead
United States
www.workstead.com
←—P. 34 ARCADE BAKERY
www.arcadebakery.com
Photos: Matthew Williams

**Yolanda Vilalta
& Helena Jaumá**
Spain
←—P. 170 CLUB RESTAURANT
BANANAS
www.bananas-barcelona.es
Photos: Xavier Ferrer

LET'S GO OUT AGAIN

INTERIORS FOR RESTAURANTS,
BARS AND
UNUSUAL FOOD PLACES

This book was conceived, edited,
and designed by Gestalten.

Edited by Michelle Galindo, Sven Ehmann,
and Robert Klanten
Text and preface by Shonquis Moreno

Cover by Jonas Herfurth
Cover photography by Richard Powers
Layout and design by Jonas Herfurth
Typefaces: BC Steiner by Vojtěch Říha,
Castledown by The Entente

Proofreading by Rachel Sampson

Printed by Eberl Print, Immenstadt/Allgäu

Made in Germany

Published by Gestalten, Berlin 2015
ISBN 978-3-89955-559-2

© Die Gestalten Verlag GmbH & Co. KG,
Berlin 2015

For more information, please visit
www.gestalten.com.

Bibliographic information published by the Deutsche
Nationalbibliothek. The Deutsche Nationalbibliothek
lists this publication in the Deutsche Nationalbiblio-
grafie; detailed bibliographic data are available online
at http://dnb.d-nb.de.

None of the content in this book was published in ex-
change for payment by commercial parties or designers;
Gestalten selected all included work based solely on its
artistic merit.

This book was printed on paper certified according to
the standard of FSC®.